Landmark
BOOKS
P9-DBV-410

Leonardo da Vinci

LEONARDO DA VINCI

BY EMILY HAHN

Illustrated by MIMI KORACH

RANDOM HOUSE · NEW YORK

Second Printing

Published in New York by Random House, Inc.
and simultaneously in Toronto, Canada, by
Random House of Canada, Limited

Library of Congress Catalog Card Number: 56-5461
Manufactured in the United States of America

To Carola Boxer

CONTENTS

1 BOY OF VINCI 3

2 YOUNG APPRENTICE IN FLORENCE 15

3 THE CRAZIEST FLORENTINE 30

4 LODOVICO IL MORO 45

5 "THE LAST SUPPER" 63

6 THE REIGN OF "THE PRINCE" 80

7 FLYING MACHINES, CANALS AND MEN 98

8 HOPE FOLLOWS DISAPPOINTMENTS 114

9 SCIENCE AND ART 130

10 "THE MEDICI MADE ME AND BROKE ME" 146

11 AT THE COURT OF FRANCIS I 167

INDEX 177

Leonardo da Vinci

Chapter 1

BOY OF VINCI

When you go to Florence, Italy, and look at the city and the rocky, hilly country around it, you may think that all of this has changed very little since the great palaces and bridges were first built. And you will be right. Those bare or olive-covered hills of Tuscany and the long empty valleys between the hill ranges are just the same. And those castles and walls, those bell towers in the distance, are not very different from the scenes the Italians looked upon five hundred years ago.

The city itself would not seem strange today to Leonardo da Vinci who lived there long ago. Of course he would notice that the old city walls have broken down and a number of houses have sprung up beyond. He would recognize the Pitti Palace, and the Medici tomb, and the workshops of the goldsmiths. He would remember the bridges and the golden glow of the stone itself. For the stone of which many of these houses are built seems, through the centuries, to have soaked in something of the hot sun of Florentine summers.

Leonardo was born in 1452 near Vinci, a village not far from Florence. He was about the same age as Christopher Columbus. If you think of them as if they belong together, you will not be wrong. They belong to the same age and shared the spirit of that age—the spirit of exploration, curiosity and desire for truth.

A stranger to our civilization might wonder why we pay such tribute to Leonardo da Vinci. He might very well ask us to show what this man has done to make us talk of him with such admiration.

I imagine that he would say, "I can understand your reverence for Columbus. He discovered the New World.

I can see why you would make a fuss about Michelangelo—there are all his statues and pictures as proof of his genius. Or Botticelli, or any of the other artists of the time. I can understand why you remember Luther, who was soon to stir up a revolt in Germany against the great Church. I can see why you would remember villains like the Borgias. All these fifteenth-century people did something, or left something, to prove how they affected the world.

"But what did Leonardo leave behind that explains all this excitement over his name? From what I can make out, he left precious little: few paintings, or bits of painting in other people's compositions—a few pieces of sculpture—evidence that he planned a great statue, but never finished it—a number of little notebooks of scribbles and sketches. That's all. Why do you honor the name of Leonardo da Vinci?"

If you look at it that way, the stranger's question is hard to answer. But the fact is, we do remember Leonardo. We do honor him for what he was, and we think of him as a greater man even than Botticelli. The world has always known he was a great man, even before his famous notebooks were gathered up and studied. His reputation began during his lifetime and has never died out, though it has had its ups and downs.

The remarkable thing about Leonardo was that he was interested in everything. Centuries before anyone else had even started to guess about many subjects, Leonardo seems to have known a good deal about them. Of course he was a great painter as well. But he didn't leave enough of his work to prove it to those who demand quantity as well as quality.

He was a very good-looking man; people who knew him said he was "the most beautiful man who ever lived." But he had no famous love affairs; he never married or had any family. Unlike so many heroes that we love to read about in America, he didn't illustrate a great success story against tremendous odds. In his lifetime he didn't have the honor he deserved.

No, those ordinary romantic stories have nothing to do with Leonardo. He was great purely because of his tremendous intellect. It was his brain that created the adventure of his life, and that adventure is still exciting today, five centuries later.

Leonardo's father was Piero da Vinci, meaning "of the village of Vinci." He was a young lawyer, son of a long line of lawyers.

Leonardo was nurtured and taught as well as any boy in the village. But it is probable that the local school was quite mediocre even though Vinci was near Florence and the new enthusiasm for learning had spread out a long way. Leonardo's father was a clever and capable lawyer, and there was much coming and going in the family between Vinci and Florence.

But the boy Leonardo wasn't a quiet, well-behaved pupil. He neglected Latin and mathematics and literature. Indeed, he seems to have preferred finding things out in his own way, at his own speed. Frequently he would slip away to climb the rocky mountains that surrounded his home. There he would gather fish and other small animals and watch the way the rivers ran.

One day, as he was to remember later, he stood for a long time staring at a layer of rock that he came across, high up in a cave in the wind-swept hills. There were shells embedded in that rock, shells he recognized as belonging to some sort of sea creature, and the bones of a big fish. Now the sea shells and bones had turned to stone, or fossils, as we call them. How had they got there, miles away from the sea and hundreds of feet above sea level? Because they were part of the rock and embedded in it, Leonardo knew no person could have brought them all that way and left them to puzzle other people.

Today we know the answer to that puzzle. That is not because we are cleverer than the people of Leonardo's day. It is because scientists have had five hundred years longer in which to observe and experiment. But nobody could explain to Leonardo about sea shells on a mountain because no one knew. Furthermore, not very many people even wondered why sea bones should be found in a mountain cave.

But Leonardo had a thirsty curiosity that noticed things like that and a quick brain that tried to work out the answers. That is why he was so remarkable a person. He had a modern brain, yet through some freak of chance he was born way back in 1452.

Probably you have heard of the Renaissance, which means "re-birth" or "renewal," as an important period in European history. It is hard to name any particular dates for the Renaissance because it happened to different countries at slightly different times, spreading slowly through the continent of Europe. We know, however, that Leonardo was born right in the middle of the Italian Renaissance. He is so much a part of it that it is sometimes hard to decide whether Leonardo's genius flourished as a result of the influence of the age, or whether he gave the Renaissance a push by being the way he was. Probably both are true.

Certainly we know that an extraordinary number of important things happened in Leonardo's time. For example, printing with movable type was invented just two years after his birth. Paper was invented, too, or at least rediscovered, at this time. You can imagine what a difference paper and printing would make to a civilization which had depended on parchment and handwriting for its books. All of a sudden books became comparatively cheap and plentiful. And those people who led the way in new thought were able to record their ideas for hundreds of others to read. With printed books, more and more people could learn about these new ideas.

While Leonardo was a young man, Copernicus was born—Copernicus, who studied the theories of the ancients and finally published his conclusion that the world was round like a ball and moved around the sun. We know that Columbus, too, believed this. In fact, many learned men did.

There were countless other investigations and theories springing up all around. Leonardo's interest in those fossils was a typical example. Probably his grandfather would not have bothered about them. There they were, he may have thought if he thought anything. How they got there would probably not have interested men of that generation. But in Leonardo's world the very air was different; it made people want to think. Science came into its own.

One of the things it seemed natural for Leonardo to try to do was paint. Nowadays it is hard for us to realize how important the arts of painting and sculpture seemed to men and women of fifteenth-century Italy. Then, drawings and paintings and sculpture not only gave pleasure to the world, but were actually necessary, for there were no cameras or photographs. The only way to record the faces of famous people or the important events of history was to paint or draw or model them.

Leonardo worked hard at his drawing. He made sketches and notes of the flowers and birds and rocks and fish that caught his eye. He was passionately interested in painting, not only in getting a scene down on canvas, but in discovering some new and better way to mix his paints. For in Leonardo's day, a good Florentine artist was responsible for the manufacture of his materials.

One of the most exciting discoveries of the Renaissance was made in the field of art. For it was at this time that artists learned what we call the rules of perspective. Until then, pictures had been drawn or painted as a child makes pictures. Artists had ignored the fact, obvious to us, that objects seen at a distance are small, and those close up seem large. Without any hesitation they painted scenes in which angels hung in the clouds like giants, as large in the distance as the saints on the ground close to the viewer's eye.

But during the Renaissance artists began to realize that two parallel lines stretching out into the distance look as if they were coming together. They began to play with the new fashion, pointing out jubilantly to each other that with careful application of the rules of perspective they could play any number of tricks. They could make their pictures look much more real.

They caught the trick of using light and shade to make rich velvet gleam on the picture as it really did in the hand. They learned to cause the limbs and face of some figure to appear as if they actually stood out on the canvas. Perspective was a wonderful new toy. In the great studios of Florence it was the chief topic of conversation among artists and their apprentices.

At home in Vinci, young Leonardo also experimented and played the new game of perspective. He was a tall, beautiful, fair-haired boy, about thirteen years old, when one day his skill tempted him to try something harder. A peasant who lived near the Vinci family came in carrying a large round piece of wood. He had cut it from a fig tree felled on his land.

"I thought this would make a nice shield, Ser Piero," he said to Leonardo's father, "because it's a good piece of wood." He was referring to the decorative paintings or colored carvings on wood that people liked to hang outside their doors, or on their walls, as a kind of coat of arms. "Do you know some painter in Florence who would do it reasonably for me? You're well acquainted in the town."

Ser Piero said amiably that he could get it done. Then he forgot all about the piece of wood, and it lay around the house until Leonardo noticed it was getting warped. He straightened it out, oiled it, polished it, saw that it was properly cured. Actually he had no special interest in it, but he was a boy who liked to work with his hands as well as his brain. Ser Piero noticed him at it and said, "You're always painting; why not have a try at turning out something useful for a change? See if you can decorate this shield in a reasonable manner."

This was a challenge. Father and son weren't getting on very well just then. This sometimes happens when a boy is growing up, and Leonardo's stepmother could hardly be expected to stand up for him. The boy took the wood into his own room and set about planning a design for it and collecting as models every queer little creature he could find in the woods and streams—lizards, crickets, snakes and bats.

Soon the dead bodies of the animals began to decay, but he was so busy at his task he paid no attention to the smell. He used different features of each for the monster he painted on the shield, copying the eyes of one, the horrid jaws of another, the tufted ears of a third. From these he portrayed a horrible dragon breathing fire. Then he covered up his window, leaving only one ray of light that fell full on the shield, and called his father to come and look at it.

Ser Piero was completely fooled because he was accustomed to the flat paintings of artists who didn't know

Young Leonardo used living animals as his models.

the secrets of perspective. He thought the dragon was alive and coming at him. In fact, he actually turned and started to run. It was a triumph for Leonardo. Never again did Ser Piero underrate his son. He bought an ordinary cheap shield in Florence for the peasant, who was very happy to have it, and sold Leonardo's work for a big sum.

This incident convinced the lawyer that Leonardo's future lay in some Florentine studio, apprenticed to one of the well-known painters there. He began making inquiries around the city.

He had new plans for himself as well, and resolved to move his household to Florence. In 1468, when Leonardo was sixteen, the whole family left Vinci and set up housekeeping in the big city.

Chapter 2

YOUNG APPRENTICE IN FLORENCE

The people of fifteenth-century Italy didn't think of themselves as Italians, because Italy wasn't a nation. What we know as one country was divided into a large number of little states. Often each one was only a city with a few extra farms and castles thrown in. Men referred to themselves as Venetians, or Romans, or Milanese, or Tuscans.

Italy was held together not by a single government, but by her position as a peninsula sticking out like a boot into the waters of the Mediterranean. The king, or duke, or lord of one state was always trying to annex another state. When he happened to be leader of one of the five biggest countries, his campaigns were something for the smaller lords to be afraid of.

Florence was supposed to be a republic, and in the past she had been governed by a body of men who presumably represented the people's will. But when the Vinci family moved inside the city walls, the city was actually under the thumb of the Medici family. Although the members didn't call themselves lords, this family was the true strong ruler of Florence.

The Medici were bankers who had made a tremendous fortune. They attained their powerful position by lending great sums to important people in the city, and outside as well—kings and dukes and Popes. From time to time, of course, other strong Florentine families tried to unseat them. But for years the Medici had kept their place and improved it.

A year after the Vinci family moved from the country, Lorenzo de Medici had succeeded to the invisible throne. Although he was only twenty-one, he seemed fully capable of hanging on to the power he had inherited. He was an acute statesman, not so good at business as his forefathers, but a man of taste and intelligence nevertheless.

Florence was a very wealthy place, specializing in the manufacture and export of cloth. There were brightly-colored woolens and every sort of luxurious material—silk and velvet and glittering brocades of gold and silver.

Next in importance to the velvets and brocades were the jewels for which Florentine goldsmiths were famous. Their cunning work was the best of its kind in Italy. They made jewels and plate for rich nobles everywhere. Even today Florentine goldsmiths are supposed to be the best in Europe.

But in Leonardo's day they didn't confine their work to pretty necklaces and brooches. Some of them were sculptors as well. And when a man was a sculptor, he often tried his hand at painting frescoes, and from there it was a natural step to painting in general.

Today we think of our painters and sculptors and architects as very special. We respect them and a good many people hold them in awe. But in the fifteenth century it was a little different. They were looked upon as workmen, or artisans, rather than as cultured artists like the poets who thronged the courts of the princes and dukes.

To be an artisan was an important role in Italian

life, however. When Piero da Vinci decided to send Leonardo as apprentice to a painter, he did it so that the youth might learn a special skill. It was a job like other jobs, one which Piero hoped would make his son independent.

We must not think of Leonardo's joining a studio in the same way that we would think of it today. In our world a person who is specially talented in music or drawing is somebody dedicated, somebody special. Leonardo had just such talents too, but it didn't make him special in his father's eyes. Piero was only interested in having his son learn a trade at small cost.

Under Lorenzo's encouragement and patronage, Florence was becoming one of the beautiful cities of the Continent. Stonecutters and workers in metal and wood, sculptors and gardeners were always at work on big estates or public buildings. The rich men of the city used their wealth to buy the best of such things that they could find. Lorenzo, like his father before him, tried to further the cause of art and literature.

In 1453, Constantinople had been captured and occupied by the Turks, and the Greek scholars who lived there had fled. Many of them escaped to Italy, where they were made welcome. Everyone became freshly interested in Greek culture. It was Lorenzo's grandfather, Cosimo de Medici, who commissioned a Florentine scholar to translate the works of Plato into Latin.

He did it so well that even today his translation is the standard one.

Lorenzo de Medici carried on the family tradition, and did his best to make the city a center of all that was best in learning and art. He himself wrote good poetry and composed songs. So you can imagine that Florence buzzed with talk about new ideas in science and art and music and architecture. It was all exciting and stimulating to a youth just arrived from the quiet countryside of Tuscany.

Looking around for the right master for his son, Ser Piero decided on Andrea del Verrocchio. This artist was well known as "one of the most highly esteemed instructors in every branch of the arts." Verrocchio was a goldsmith, sculptor and painter. Like many of his colleagues he had had his training with a goldsmith whose name, after the custom of the time, he adopted.

Piero da Vinci showed some of Leonardo's sketches to Verrocchio. The artist-teacher immediately realized that they were the work of someone with rare talent, and accepted Leonardo as an apprentice. Of course Piero had to pay a fee since that was the way apprenticeships were arranged. The sixteen-year-old youth moved into the master's house and immediately set to work.

Leonardo found himself among busy companions. Verrocchio was an industrious man, and his pupils imitated him. Their work was more than sketching first "from the cast" as we do today in art schools, and then daubing for a while at a few refined still lifes. Verrocchio's pupils had to study more than the art of putting paint on canvas, or clay on a framework. They had to master the secrets of manufacturing the paint itself, and the structure of the statue's framework as well.

Until Leonardo's time paintings had been done in "tempera," a kind of water color which faded quickly. Now artists were trying out the effect of mixing their pigments with various sorts of oil, for oil kept the color bright and fresh. There were also hundreds of problems to settle arising from that great discovery, perspective.

Over and above these workmanlike interests of the studio, Verrocchio, like many another Florentine, was keenly interested in the new knowledge of mathematics. To an artist, mathematics was important as a natural outgrowth of the modern attempt to paint realistically. Verrocchio didn't know much about geometry, for example, but he was determined to learn. As Leonardo watched the older man at his books, he determined to follow his master's example. He would make up for all the studying he had neglected at school. So now, rather late in the day, he started acquiring a knowledge of mathematics.

Leonardo studied everything else, too, that came his

way through the widespread interests of Verrocchio —medicine, astronomy, machinery, and even geology. When he read about rocks and fossils, he remembered the sea shells and fish bones he had seen in the mountain cave. At last he began to understand how they came to be there! As he read and studied, he continued to write in his notebooks, in a combination of reminders and diary entries. "How many kings, how many peoples, how many changes of states and various events have happened," he wrote, "since the wondrous form of this fish came to its end in the dark recess of that cave."

These notebooks are the most regular record that we have of Leonardo's mind. In spite of the hundreds of years between us, they show how eager he was for knowledge and how many sides there were to his character. He put down all sorts of bits and pieces as they popped into his mind—poems that he had read and liked, poems that he himself wrote, reminders to ask this or that man to teach him something, little scoldings to himself.

In some of the entries, you can see traces of his lawyer father's character, for now and then Leonardo seems to have been possessed of a businesslike spirit. He would note down what things cost, and the occasion on which he had spent the money. Or he would give a list of the colors in a scene of which he had just made a pen drawing. The machinery that was beginning to fascinate him was diagrammed in the notebooks, with labels and descriptions.

One of the most interesting things about all this is that Leonardo made his notes *backwards.* He wrote in what is called mirror writing, because you can read it only by holding it up to a mirror. Why he did it is a question. We know that he was left-handed as well as right-handed. He was one of those rare people who can use either hand equally well. But he may have used mirror writing to keep what he wrote secret from any casual eye. Though it is easy enough to figure out Leonardo's notes if you work at it, you can't read them at a glance. Perhaps that is what he wanted. Think of how hard it would be for you to write everything backwards! Yet Leonardo seems to have done it at a perfectly normal speed.

When a master like Verrocchio was given a commission, or order, to do a large painting or statue, it was understood that his pupils would help him. Life in the master's house was much like life in a boarding school today. The young men became friends and had their jokes and their work together.

Leonardo began to enjoy himself, not only because he loved to work and learn things, but because for the first time he found himself among companions his own age. He made a great impression on them too. Often in the writings of other painters of the time you come across some mention of Leonardo. One will refer to his great beauty, another to his high spirits, another to his talents and so on. He was one of those people who are always doing things to amuse others. We might call him a show-off; at least, he was a born entertainer. He wrote songs, he made musical instruments which he played himself, delighting in inventing new forms.

But most of the day he and his friends were helping the master with statues, or architectural jobs, or painting. Leonardo did so well and enjoyed his work so much that he continued to stay in Verrocchio's house long beyond the period of his apprenticeship. In fact, he was still there when he was twenty-six years old.

During that time he did a great deal of work, not simply because he was told to, but because like the master and the other men he loved it. He thrilled over experiments with new materials and new techniques. When Verrocchio was carving a statuary group, his pupil might produce the cherubs peeking over their shoulders. Or he would produce bits and pieces of paintings. Leonardo learned how to apply ornamentation to

A tourney meant a great procession through the city.

roofs inside and out. As he worked, he picked up all sorts of tricks of the trade, and invented some new ones, too.

One of the tasks given the studio as a whole was to design costumes for a tournament. Lorenzo de Medici had decreed this tournament, or tourney, as a celebration for a double event: the end of a local war, and the

Jeweled costumes flashed as the noblemen rode by.

finish of a plague epidemic. The plague was something that these Italians expected every year when the hot weather started. To escape the plague rich people got out of town whenever possible, until the plague season was over.

This tourney took place in the winter when the sickness abated. Lorenzo gave people as much in the way of splendid spectacles as possible, because they loved to watch processions. And a tourney meant a great procession through the city with all the nobles dressed in the most gorgeous clothes that could be dreamed of.

Leonardo and the other pupils of Verrocchio threw themselves into this work. The young artists must have felt very proud when they saw the Medici brothers, Lorenzo and the younger Giuliano, and all the nobles and millionaires and visiting notables, dressed in their gold and silver and precious stones and embroidery encrusted with pearls. The jewels and costumes flashed and gleamed and glowed as the noblemen rode majestically between the stone palaces of Florence. It was a fairy-tale scene. Artists loved Florence because Lorenzo knew how to put on a show.

We can imagine what it must have been like because so many of their paintings are of processions like this. They show horses with bejeweled trappings, carrying young princes along the curving roads of Tuscany. In the background are flowery mountain slopes, with castles topping the steep peaks in the distance. The bright clear air, filled with Italian sunshine, was enough to make any man feel that he could paint, and Leonardo really could.

But this happy existence had its cruel side as well. Lorenzo, the young Medici ruler, made enemies. It was natural that he should have them even if he had been the most tactful man in Florence, and he wasn't that. There was a family called the Pazzi who hated him. Lorenzo kept getting in their way in business, and at last they determined to put an end to him. It was easy for them to find allies. Many other members of famous families were willing to help.

The plan was to put an end to the Medici altogether by killing both Lorenzo and his young brother Giuliano. The date they selected was April 26, 1478. On that day a number of assassins came into the big cathedral, called the Duomo, while the two young men were attending High Mass, and set upon them. Giuliano was mortally wounded. But Lorenzo, who was a good swordsman, fought off the assassins and escaped into the sacristy.

The conspirators had counted on killing both Medici and taking over their power in full view of the people. But with Lorenzo still alive the conspirators were made to pay dearly for their attempt. Some of them were hanged in full view of the populace, out of the windows of the Palazzo Vecchio (which you can still see today, exactly as it was then), and the bodies were left there as a warning. Others were cut to pieces and thrown into the river Arno. Eighty people in all lost their lives that day.

But one, a principal assassin, had escaped. Bernardo de Bandino Baroncelli had not run out of the Duomo when the others did. Instead he made his way up the bell tower and hid there, crouching under the bells. When the fuss had died down, he was able to sneak out. He wasn't caught for another year and a half.

In those days painters did the work we expect of photographers today. The men who ran Florence wanted a picture—as it were, a photograph—of the victims of this execution, to keep as a warning to all possible wrongdoers of the future. They gave the assignment to Botticelli, an artist whose name is familiar to us, as the painter of "Primavera." He was commissioned to decorate the tower of the chief magistrate's palace with portraits of the hanged men. He was well paid for his work, which can still be seen today.

Leonardo heard of this transaction with longing. Though he was twenty-six and had already made a considerable name for himself, he was out of luck and rather poor. It is not certain, but we can be fairly sure that he was not on good terms with his father, for he was still living in Verrocchio's house. Piero da Vinci's second wife had died. Now he had married for the third time, and this wife had at last given him a son. Probably Piero had lost interest in Leonardo.

Then, in December of the following year, Bernardo de Bandino Baroncelli was caught and brought to justice and hanged. Leonardo went and drew a sketch of the body in order to submit it to the men who were commissioning paintings of the murderers. Botticelli got the job, not Leonardo; but the sketch still exists with its careful, businesslike notes. They give us a feeling of shock, that anyone could have been so practical about a subject like that.

"Small cap tan-colored," he wrote, "doublet of black satin, black lined jerkin, blue coat lined with the throats of foxes and the collar of the coat lined with black and white stripes of velvet. Bernardo de Bandino Baroncelli. Black hose."

Chapter 3

THE CRAZIEST FLORENTINE

Leonardo never seemed to feel himself a part of events around him. It was a time when other Florentines were very much excited about the quarrels of the Medici. Ordinarily they weren't people who got excited easily; they liked to attend to the peaceful business of making and buying and selling. But the violence of the Pazzi attempt to overthrow the Medici and the resulting executions were bound to have an aftereffect.

Friends of the Pazzi family, including the Pope at Rome, determined to bring down the haughty Lorenzo before he should become more powerful. They began an intrigue with the King of Naples. He sent out an army to conquer Florence, in league with the papal army. Because the citizens of Florence hated and feared war, they were very much worried. Lorenzo engaged a military engineer to prepare a defense of the city.

Only recently had firearms come into common use. Most armies were equipped with big guns and cannon that seemed terrible to the people who were threatened by them. Nowadays we would consider them almost harmless, of course.

Leonardo was fascinated with such weapons. The murderous reason for these engines, the use to which they would be put, never bothered him at all. He was interested in them simply because they were so efficient.

He made a lot of designs and plans and sketches of gun carriages and the manufacture of the guns themselves. He invented a cannon that had no "kick" in firing, and a machine gun as well. Actually, none of these was ever constructed. At least no historian has ever mentioned them. We know Leonardo wasn't hired by Lorenzo, but that didn't keep him from designing the things. He loved the exercise for its own sake; he loved to use his brain. We still have the plans and sketches to prove that Leonardo was many hundreds of years ahead of his age in mechanical ability.

By the time Leonardo was twenty-seven, his paintings had gained him a tremendous reputation. He started a fashion of painting Madonnas like living, breathing mothers. He produced two beautiful holy groups that were so much admired that all the other painters of Florence began to imitate his style.

But although the public admitted that his work was wonderful, they also alleged, truthfully, that Leonardo was a most unsatisfactory man to do business with. He was never in a hurry. Time meant nothing at all to him if he saw a chance to do the work better. He would let a painting wait for weeks, months, or years if necessary, while he experimented with a new method of grinding pigments or preparing a surface.

When a pretty young woman wanted her portrait painted, she wanted it within a reasonable length of time. If Leonardo kept her waiting until she got a lot older, she naturally complained about him to her friends.

And in other ways, too, Leonardo was difficult. He would accept an advance payment for materials for some job, and then take so long over the job that his client lost patience and gave it out again to some other artist. Leonardo couldn't return the money because he had spent it on the materials. This probably explains why so many of his clever inventions weren't carried out in practice. No careful Florentine merchant would trust Leonardo to deliver the goods.

For these reasons Lorenzo de Medici held off and didn't order things from him. In any case, the war was settled before many mechanical engines were put to the test, no matter who designed them. The papal troops chased the Florentine army almost to the gates of the city. By this time, Leonardo had worked out wonderful engines for the defense of the walls, which of course were never made or used. But after the papal troops had taken one fortress within eight miles of Florence, they declared a three-month truce, to rest the men.

The armies of these Italian states were not raised as ours are, by seeking volunteers or drafting. Princes hired mercenary soldiers to do their fighting. To be a mercenary soldier in Italy was a career like any other; you agreed to fight for your master, and as long as he paid you, you did so. The fighting was not awfully fierce. Mercenary troops did a lot of marching about, and their sieges were pretty easy going. They preferred not to use heavy guns if they could get out of it, because it was hard work carting them around. But little by little, guns became so popular that they had to have them.

Sometimes, in the middle of a battle, a mercenary on one side would find himself in combat with some other mercenary who in the war before had been fighting next to him as a comrade. In the circumstances, as you can imagine, these engagements did not result in much bloodshed. After a battle the winning side usually freed the prisoners taken from the losing side, just because they didn't know what else to do with them.

Now in the course of this war against Florence, Lorenzo de Medici decided that the truce gave him a chance to bring the whole thing to an end. Very courageously, he went to Naples and talked it all over with the King of Naples. As a result they made a settlement, and peace returned to Florence. For the moment Leonardo found no more stimulation to his talent for designing firearms. Everyone was satisfied, for the people of that day were as terrified of their sort of war as we are of ours today.

Peace brought a rush of work for the artists of the city. That is, for everybody but Leonardo. The more celebrated his painting became, the less inclined were people to risk ordering anything from him. We still have several paintings of this phase. Each was carried through far enough to show how marvelous it would have been if it had been completed. Always, before it was finished, Leonardo decided that he was not satisfied, that the groundwork was not good enough. So he would abandon it in order to work harder at his preparations for another picture.

Leonardo may have understood why more work didn't come his way, but that did not make the fact any the less bitter. Other men with only half his talent had become rich and honored. Leonardo resented this. Finally his resentment went so far that he began to hate Florence and especially Lorenzo de Medici. For in spite of his famous appreciation of art, Lorenzo had never commissioned Leonardo to do any work for him.

Leonardo disliked the famous scholars of Florence, too—those philosophers who spent hours discussing the processes of the mind and the nature of truth. As an artist he felt contempt for people who never worked with their hands, and used only their minds. He knew how to figure out the way things worked. But he could also make the things to prove his theories. Why shouldn't they? Yet they prospered and he did not. They were appreciated and he was not. In his notebook he wrote:

"They go about, puffed up and pompous, in fine raiment and bejewelled, not from the fruits of their own labors but from those of others; my own labors they refuse to recognize. They despise me, the inventor, yet how much more are they to blame for not being inventors, but trumpeters and reciters of the work of others. They are little indebted to nature, for it is only by the chance that they wear clothes that they can be distinguished from herds of animals."

Poor Leonardo! At last he made up his mind to take an important step and leave Florence altogether. He would go to Milan, in the north.

Artists of the fifteenth century depended on rich people even more than ours do today. In effect, they had to hire themselves out to private persons. They became attached to the family of some great house. It was not like being a servant exactly, but it was something like it.

A rich man who took on the responsibility of an artist would pay for a certain number of his creations. He would try to help him by showing off his work to other rich people. Now and then he might give him a present on the side. Such rich men were called "patrons," and the artist who got a generous patron was considered lucky. As we have seen, Leonardo had never yet acquired a useful friend like this. However, when he thought of his great talent, he felt that he should have rated the leading patron in Florence, Lorenzo de Medici himself.

Now that Leonardo had decided to move to Milan —no small decision in those days—he must arrange some contact with a powerful man in the new city. For once he was fortunate, or seemed to be, because he had a letter of introduction and a visit to pay to Lodovico Sforza, the ruler of Milan. He was called Lodovico il Moro, or Lodovico the Moor, because of his swarthy complexion. Legally speaking, Lodovico wasn't really the ruler. He was only the regent for his young nephew the Duke, Gian Galeazzo Sforza. But Lodovico had every intention of getting rid of Gian Galeazzo someday soon. *He* was the strong man of the family.

Lorenzo de Medici did not at all mind recommending the painter he had snubbed. Like the rest of Florence he admired Leonardo's work, on the infrequent occasions when he saw any. Just now the artist had succeeded in catching Lorenzo's eye and, for once, winning his approval, by the invention of one of those gadgets at which he excelled.

It was a new kind of lyre, or lute, made of silver. It was shaped like a horse's skull. The teeth served as pegs for the strings of the lute and were turned for tuning. It was a clever gadget and a true novelty. Lorenzo determined to send it as a present from himself to Lodovico, who was his ally in matters of war. Then Lodovico would see how clever Florentine artists were.

So Leonardo left Florence early in 1482, with no regrets and with high hopes of his new venture.

Like Florence, Milan was a rich and beautiful city. Also like Florence, a lot of its wealth was based on the textile industry, though the Milanese were famous armorers, too. The people of the countryside raised mulberry trees and silkworms, and the city looms fashioned the loveliest of shimmering silks. Milanese silks and woolens were exported far and wide.

But there all resemblance between the cities ceased. It was not only a difference in the surrounding landscape; the Tuscan hills were here replaced by the Lombardy plain. But the attitude toward craftsmanship and art was different.

Florence was traditionally the home of sculptors, painters, architects and musicians. Under the encouragement of the Medici, these people grew more famous and prosperous year by year. Leonardo was an exception. As we have seen, this was partly his own fault for being so particular about his work.

In Milan, people of his sort were very poorly paid. Besides, the Milanese artists were not so eager as the Florentines, nor so adept, nor so generous and ready to accept ideas from outside. Any craftsman who knew his work, no matter where he came from, was welcomed in Florence; but in Milan the artisans were terribly jealous of outsiders, and objected to using them in any way. Often laborers refused to build a palace or a cathedral because it had not been designed by a Milanese—and this even though no Milanese had been found capable of designing the building properly.

It was an attitude of mind that seemed very strange to the always-inquiring Leonardo da Vinci. And it did not help him at all in the difficult first days of his residence in Milan.

Lodovico himself didn't care much for impersonal art. He loved the good things of life, but he preferred rich clothes and highly flavored food and wine and the biggest jewels he could find to wall paintings and intricate large-scale inventions. The only pictures he cared for were family portraits.

It is typical of Lodovico that the task he thought Leonardo might fulfill was a gigantic conception. He wanted a great statue of his father, Francesco Sforza, former ruler of Milan, mounted on horseback. The creation of such an unwieldy monument had already baffled several Milanese. Nevertheless they opposed Leonardo's name when he was suggested. For this reason and also because great lords are often dilatory, Lodovico did not tell Leonardo during their first conversation that he wanted the Florentine to go ahead with the job. Instead he asked what sort of thing this stranger could do well.

Thereupon, Leonardo drew up a paper listing his talents and powers. It is an amazing piece of work. It seems too boastful at first glance, but as you study it you realize that Leonardo was telling what seemed to him to be the truth. At the same time he was making himself appear to be as useful as possible, trying to "sell himself," but with facts he could prove. He illustrated a lot of his propositions, and it is from this paper as much as anything else that we can appreciate how very far ahead of every other scientist he was.

"1. I have methods of construction of very light and strong bridges," he wrote, "which can be transported with the greatest ease, offering the means of pursuing an enemy and also, if necessary, of fleeing from him; and others which are safe and immune from damage from fire or in an engagement, and are at the same time easy to take to pieces and set up again. I also know how to fire and destroy the bridges of the enemy." Leonardo had invented a method of expandable bridges, and illustrated it to show the reader.

"2. In laying siege to a fortress I know how to empty the water out of moats, and how to construct . . . siege bridges, mantlets, scaling-ladders, and other instruments . . ."

He added a number of suggestions to make it easier

In his notebooks were sketches of many war machines

to scale a wall with climbing-irons, storming-ladders, and roofs on wheels that could protect the attackers.

He recommended underground passages in which to place mines under a fortress. Or, he said, if there was a river handy you could change its course and send it against the enemy. Nobody else had thought of that. He continued with his list; he had invented new light bombards, or guns. He invented fire bombs like one that was actually produced and used nearly four hundred years later. Leonardo's was never produced. In fact, most of his machinery existed only in diagram, on parchment or paper.

He invented a number of other things that mankind was to discover again long, long years afterwards. Leonardo thought up something like the shrapnel bomb, and a flame thrower, and a hand grenade. He invented a wagon covered with armor; in other words, a tank. He drew a picture of this, as well as a terrible machine with revolving scythes meant to cut people to pieces. He thought up a breech-loading gun to take the place of the muzzle-loaders everybody used. Fortunately, no one put any of these theories into practice, so the world was spared such horrors for a few more centuries.

Leonardo was not bloodthirsty. Nobody could have been less so. It was only that machinery and its uses fascinated him so much that he forgot the ultimate aim of these inventions. He could contribute peaceful ideas too, but he wanted to impress Lodovico with the idea that he was a very good man to have around in case of war—and war was a commonplace hazard in Milan. He discovered the power of steam, though no steam cannons were made after his suggestions. He even thought of a sort of poison gas, in powder form.

After enumerating all these weapons for killing, he came to his last entry: "In time of peace I think I can give the best of satisfaction, well bearing comparison with anyone else, in architecture, in the designing of buildings, whether public or private, and in the conducting of water from one place to another.

". . . I shall carry out sculptures, in marble, bronze, and clay, and similarly paintings, of every possible kind, to stand comparison with anyone else, be he who he may.

"It will also be possible to put in hand the bronze horse, which will be an immortal glory and eternal honor to the happy memory of your honored father and of the illustrious house of Sforsa. And if any of the aforesaid works should appear to anyone to be impossible of execution, I am ready at any time to put it to the test in your park or at whatever place shall be convenient to Your Excellency, to whom I most humbly commend myself."

No wonder Lodovico ignored this extraordinary letter! How could he have brought himself to believe even half of it? There wasn't any prophet to tell him that these wonders would indeed be made and used centuries in the future. He probably tossed the thing aside and said to his courtiers that Leonardo da Vinci was the craziest Florentine he had ever encountered, and laughed as he said it.

Chapter 4

LODOVICO IL MORO

As the days went on, Leonardo realized that he was being ignored in Milan just as he had been in Florence. In fact it was worse. There in his own city they had at least admired his work and copied it, on the rare occasions when there was a new Leonardo painting to copy.

He hadn't made any money out of this kind of compliment, but Leonardo actually didn't care for money at all, except when he needed it to buy new materials or to feed and clothe his assistants. (An artist who kept his own studio and had apprentices, or pupils, had to behave like a father to them. It was his duty to take care of them.)

We can tell from his notebooks exactly how Leonardo lived, because he put down everything in the notebook accounts. He ate very sparingly and almost never drank the wines that his Milanese neighbors were so fond of.

No, money didn't tempt Leonardo. What he wanted with all his heart and never got enough of was recognition and praise. He wanted honor and fame just as much as the Milanese longed for jewels and beautiful clothing. The Milanese couldn't understand his point of view.

For a long time Leonardo lived on the hope that Lodovico would tell him to go ahead on the bronze statue of Francesco Sforza, but no word came. Instead, he heard around the town that Lodovico had a very bad reputation for being stingy with artists. The Moor would pay his musicians pretty well, and his tailors and architects, but he seemed to grudge paying painters and sculptors even when he owed them money.

In the meantime, Leonardo didn't even have a bad debt to collect on, because Lodovico hadn't ordered anything, and until he did the courtiers would not show any eagerness for the new painter's work.

Leonardo was running out of the money he had saved up in Florence. Even he, with his simple tastes, needed some to go on with. Men in his position in Milan usually got together in a partnership with some other needy artist, to cut down expenses. That is what Leonardo finally did. He moved into a studio with a painter named Ambrogio de Predis, and then things went a little better.

Ambrogio was industrious and businesslike, though he wasn't much of a painter, and he found work for both of them. He was glad of the chance to work close to the famous Leonardo, and from him learned a lot about painting. As long as the partnership continued, Ambrogio painted much better than usual, especially as Leonardo sometimes gave him a hand.

The two men, with Ambrogio's brother who was a woodcarver, were soon given an important order for an altarpiece with a carved wood framework. The contract gave them more than a year to do the work, and two hundred ducats in payment.

Leonardo had been in Milan for almost a year, but the unwary monks who made the bargain didn't realize how hard it was to pin him down to any sort of time limit. Had everybody known that, Leonardo might have starved to death. But in this commission as in many to follow, his neglected contracts were pulled into shape in the end by his associate. Ambrogio de Predis would take the rough sketch or background that Leonardo had done before he lost patience with it, fill it in with his own inferior work, and get it ready for the purchaser. More and more work came the way of the shared studio.

Fortunately the Milanese were fond of at least one sort of painting; like Lodovico, they dearly liked family portraits. So Leonardo and Ambrogio stayed together in their strange but profitable partnership. They produced a number of half-and-half portraits and began to prosper.

Leonardo was thirty when he came to Milan. He lingered there year after year, waiting to be recognized as he should have been, for a genius. Still Lodovico made him wait.

But Leonardo never stopped trying to learn, and his busy pen went on writing as it went on drawing. He corresponded with friends in Florence. In his spare time, he drew sketches of the ugliest people he could find in the streets of Milan. He would work over and over these drawings to show just how skin arranges itself on a toothless mouth, or a hideous nose juts out from a face. He also wrote a long, imaginative description of a catastrophe in the Orient, all made up out of the ancient books he studied to learn something of the history of the world. He drew landscapes to illustrate the tale, so detailed and sure that for a long time people believed he had really made a voyage to the East. But at that time Leonardo had never left Italy.

So he filled his days and scraped up a living, sharing a studio with Ambrogio whose work he had secret contempt for, until he had been seven whole years in Milan. Then at last some recognition came his way.

It seems strange that this man with his magnificent brain, who had already foreseen many of the mechanical wonders that other men would not appreciate for generations to come, should have to depend for appreciation on his aptitude for designing toys. Yet that is the truth.

The Milanese nobles loved a chance to give big parties. They now had the excuse for one of the biggest celebrations in their history. Their nominal ruler, the young Duke Gian Galeazzo, was married to a girl from the ruling house of Naples. Her name was Isabella of Aragon.

It fell to Leonardo's lot to decorate the ducal castle for the celebration. It was a grim building of dark red stone. He contrived a method by which a colonnade of living green twigs ran through the courtyard, with a roof over the whole made of gilded leaves.

Immediately his reputation improved, for hundreds of wedding guests admired this marvel. Lodovico felt proud of him and began to entrust him with more commissions. Leonardo had many other tricks up his sleeve for the rest of the wedding celebrations, but the parties were interrupted and postponed by the death of Isabella's mother, and such frivolous matters were set aside.

By the time the mourning period was over, Leonardo was happy about something else. At last he was embarked on a really important project, the thing he had been longing to do—the giant bronze horse statue of Francesco Sforza.

For years this memorial had been discussed and entrusted to earlier sculptors, but nothing had come of it. Leonardo wanted to make it the greatest of its sort ever seen. Lodovico hemmed and hawed over the artist's ideas. Because Leonardo himself hemmed and hawed so much, "the Moor" doubted his ability to carry out such grand ambitions. For a while Lodovico even looked around secretly for somebody more dependable.

If he had known about this, Leonardo would have

been in despair. Instead, he was in a frenzy of getting ready, going around Milan studying horses, sketching horses, thinking horses, and wondering how on earth to balance a great weight of bronze in the way he wanted.

He planned to model his horse rearing up on its hind legs. He wanted to make it enormous, and use as much as a hundred thousand pounds of bronze—no small weight to balance on a horse's slender legs even when those too were of bronze. Should he rest the forelegs on a tree? That would look clumsy. A fallen soldier? That would be better.

In the end Lodovico did not betray Leonardo after all, for a lucky accident put him out of the idea. Gian Galeazzo and Isabella came back after a year's mourning. Again Leonardo was set to work getting ready for a great ball in Isabella's honor. The horse would have to wait.

Italians have always loved costume balls, and this was to be a masquerade. It must have been a wonderful one to watch. Isabella opened the ball with a Neapolitan dance, wearing a gold brocade gown and a stiff white satin cloak. Then there were more set dances and pageants. Everyone was magnificently dressed, many according to Leonardo's designs.

At midnight one end of the hall was revealed by the raising of the curtain. For a moment there was complete silence. Everyone gazed at the scene. Then wild applause swept the room. Leonardo had surpassed himself!

He had constructed a great hemisphere of deep blue to represent the heavens. There was a mountain peak on one side—Mount Olympus. It was supposed to be nighttime, and the sky was dark except for the stars. Leonardo had made real stars, arranged in the forms of the Zodiac as they were thought to be in the sky. He had the seven planets moving in their orbits, and the moon. With these stars all the constellations kept twinkling, because he had lights running along behind them, moving back and forth by machinery.

Then a classical drama was acted out. Figures floated down from Mount Olympus—gods and goddesses. All the while, a choir kept singing music that pleased the ears of the guests while it drowned out the noise of the machinery backstage. Leonardo had constructed this machinery on a new method of gearings.

There were dances and songs and a poem written and declaimed especially for Isabella, the guest of honor. This was the accepted way of showing courtesy. The party became known as the Paradise Festival, and was remembered in Milan and in other states for years to come.

It all may sound rather childish to us, because we are used to great spectacles in our theaters. But it was new to the world then. Leonardo couldn't have minded doing it, because he loved making anything mechanical and putting his theories to the test. Besides, the triumph of that festival pleased Lodovico il Moro so much that he committed himself at last to being Leonardo's patron. There was no more talk of finding someone else to make the bronze statue of Francesco.

Leonardo was able to move out of Ambrogio's studio and set up for himself in Lodovico's great castle. There he had all the space he wanted. Not only was he given living quarters and a studio, but he also had the use of a big room at the top of the castle. Here he carried out all the work he wanted to do on secret experiments. He was allowed to lock up the great room when he wasn't there. He was officially Lodovico's court painter.

That year of 1490, Lodovico took Leonardo to Pavia, a city under the control of the Sforzas, to give his expert advice on the cathedral they were building there. Lodovico's brother was a cardinal and it was his cathedral, so the Sforzas were especially interested. Nothing much ever came of Leonardo's work on the cathedral, but the trip was good for him. Never before had he been anywhere except his own village of Vinci and Florence and Milan.

Pavia's castle possessed a famous library, to which

many scholars came from distant places. The court painter had the run of it, and he spent long hours studying its books. Leonardo was always conscious of not having a good education. He confessed that he felt like an uneducated boor in the presence of really learned men. So now that he had the chance, he devoured as much learning as he could. And when he went back to his experiment chamber in Milan, he carried on with his tests and theories with even greater enthusiasm.

For weeks he was fascinated by architectural questions. No doubt the problem of the Pavia cathedral set him off, and once Leonardo got started on a train of thought he would continue for a long time, pursuing it to the end. He planned largely, even wildly. He dreamed up a new kind of city in layers, rather like giant skyscrapers. All the rich aristocrats were to live in the upper regions, away from the noise and work and smells which were much in evidence in the fifteenth century. The hard jobs of life were to be carried on down below by the inferior classes. Needless to say, this city existed only on paper.

After coming back from Pavia, however, Leonardo got started on the study of light. He had found a book about it which made him think again about the theory which everyone accepted until then. People had decided that their eyes sent out rays to whatever they were looking at. These rays then returned to the eye with the image, which was passed on to the soul. Leonardo had thought so too, but suddenly he decided it couldn't be that way. He wrote, "It is impossible that the eye should send out from itself, by means of the visual rays, the faculty of vision."

So Leonardo got to work playing games with light. He stumbled on the experiment which we now know well, taking a piece of paper and making a tiny hole in it, and watching how light travels in straight lines and comes out of the hole in a cone. He figured out why images will be upside down unless a lens corrects the position of the light rays.

From there it was a short step to the study of the eye itself and its lens. For about a year Leonardo had already been making anatomical studies, dissecting dead bodies. His drawings of these experiments are among his most exact and beautiful.

One of the ways in which he immediately used his new knowledge of light and reflection was the construction of a lamp with which he could work at night. Other people toiled away at night in a dim shade. They could do very little after the sun had gone down, for they depended on a dismal little wick burning in a pot of oil. Leonardo took a big glass globe like a fish bowl and put a glass cylinder inside. He filled the globe with water, and in the cylinder he put the olive-oil lamp with its little wick. Thus the flame was magnified through the water, and he had a splendid light.

In his improved position, Leonardo had many requests to take in pupils as apprentices. He did so willingly, but one apprentice was to give him almost more trouble than he was worth. In fact, the boy Giacomo was worth almost nothing, strictly speaking, because his father was too poor to pay his apprentice's fee. However, Leonardo found the boy very useful as a model; he looked exactly like the kind of youth the painter liked to portray. So Leonardo took in Giacomo and outfitted him with clothes, keeping a careful account of what it cost him. Of course he never submitted a bill to anybody, but it was his nature to keep a record.

Giacomo was always stealing, and was such a nuisance to the other pupils that he became famous just for that. He stayed on at the studio for years, until he was a man, serving as an apprentice and a servant as well. All the while he pilfered and begged for clothes. Leonardo complained, all through the years, but gave him what he wanted and never kicked him out.

Those were busy days for a court painter. By this time Lodovico was making plans for his marriage to the very young Beatrice d'Este who lived at Pavia. And of course he called on Leonardo to furnish the festival trimmings with new ideas and gorgeous costumes.

Beatrice arrived in January, 1491. In honor of her coming Lodovico ordered all the armorers who had shops along the street down which she was to ride to put out their weapons and suits of armor. The bride rode down an avenue of dummy horses clad in glittering mail, on which sat visored knights in empty armor, brandishing their weapons. The main event of the wedding time was a great tourney, and for this Leonardo furnished a masque.

At first Beatrice was bored and unhappy in her marriage. As she was only fifteen, she turned to idle amusements to fill in the time. She acquired a poet laureate, and at her request he wrote various little dramatic pieces—a play, some masques and so on. For these, too, Leonardo was expected to furnish tricks and surprises.

He also found himself doing something new: he became one of the storytellers of the castle, whiling away the evenings with little fables which he worked on very hard in advance. He found a lot of these allegories in the ancient books he was so fond of ransacking. Then he furbished them up and used them on the courtiers. They were rather simple stories, and always had a moral.

To this highly intelligent man, the evenings he spent with the sort of empty-headed people who gathered around the Sforzas must have felt a bit like running a nursery school. But Leonardo took his duties as entertainer as seriously as he did all his other tasks. He was no fashionable beau. His flattery of the duchess Beatrice was rather clumsy and awkward, but he did his duty in that way too, because it was expected of him.

Games and storytelling didn't leave Leonardo a great deal of leisure. Nevertheless, he found time to go on with his work on the great bronze horse. Of course he was slow about it, but then Leonardo was always slow.

The making of a metal statue calls for a lot of preliminary work. First, you model your figure in some kind of soft material like clay; Leonardo used clay for his. To begin with he made a little model to submit for Lodovico's approval. Then he made the gigantic statue, still in clay, and it was put up on show in the castle courtyard so that the public could see what a magnificent monument it was going to be when it was finished. But the hardest part of making the statue was still ahead of him—the casting.

First Leonardo would have to cover the whole statue with another sort of plaster and let it harden. Then he must carefully remove the original clay from this shell, so that the space inside was the exact reverse of the statue's shape. This opening would then be filled with hundreds of pounds of melted bronze.

You can imagine how difficult all this would be with a big statue. When it hardened, he would have to take off the shell. If all went well, he would then have his bronze statue, a perfect copy of the original. If all did not go well, the whole thing would be ruined and would have to be done again from the beginning.

Lodovico was very proud of the clay model. As it happened, it was ready just at the time that he had arranged to marry off his niece to Maximilian I, the German who later became Emperor of the Holy Roman Empire. Lodovico was giving this niece, Bianca Maria, a very big dowry. This was because he wanted Maximilian to be an ally in the action he was planning to undertake, to get control of Gian Galeazzo's inheritance.

Ever since he married Beatrice, Lodovico had been more and more anxious to take the young Duke's place. Beatrice was extremely jealous of Isabella of

The bride rode down an avenue of dummy horses.

Aragon. She could not be happy, she said, until she and her husband had supplanted the young couple. Therefore, Lodovico gave his niece Bianca a marvelous trousseau and a wedding send-off that had every sort of attraction. Among all the wonders of the wed-

ding, the most impressive was that giant horse and rider looming over the little human beings who came to look at it.

Everyone who visited Milan for the celebration took back the news of the great horse to his own city. The name of Leonardo da Vinci was at last on everybody's tongue, as its owner had always known it should be.

Chapter 5

"THE LAST SUPPER"

As Lodovico's determination to take the ducal throne from his nephew became stronger, he asked the king of France to help him. This king, Charles VIII, was a silly, romantic young man with a head full of glorious visions.

Through his mother's family he had a vague claim to Naples, which was ruled by Isabella's father, Alfonso of Aragon. If King Charles VIII should get rid of Alfonso, then Lodovico wouldn't be afraid to kick out Isabella and Gian Galeazzo.

So Lodovico wrote letters to King Charles VIII, encouraging him to think of himself as a great general and crusader. Charles was very pious. He even planned that when he had captured Naples he would use it as headquarters and from there set out to recapture Constantinople for Christendom.

In 1494, the French King crossed the Alps at the head of the most magnificent army ever seen in Italy. Leonardo was able to admire their smart uniforms and weapons. King Charles moved unimpeded across the Sforza country on his way down the boot of Italy. On the way he interviewed his allies, Lodovico and Beatrice. He even met Isabella of Aragon at the bedside of her husband who had suddenly fallen ill. Isabella knew that her father, who was not much of a warrior, would never be able to withstand the French. She begged Charles to spare her family and give up the venture, but Charles couldn't be induced to relinquish his ambition. He continued the triumphal march. Sure enough, Alfonso fled. Naples fell to the French without a shot.

Isabella's ill fortune continued. Her husband Gian

Galeazzo died and left her and the two children at the mercy of Lodovico. Gian Galeazzo's death seemed so convenient for Lodovico that everybody was sure the young Duke had been poisoned. But there was no proof, and nobody knows for certain, even now. In those times diseases like typhoid and malaria often struck suddenly, after a patient had eaten unwisely or had been staying in mosquito-haunted country. As people had no other explanation, they blamed almost every quick death on poison.

Whether Lodovico had helped to kill his nephew or not, he wasted no time putting on a show of grief. By every rule Gian Galeazzo's little son should have followed him as the next duke. But Lodovico had had quite enough of acting as regent. This time he wanted the title for himself. He persuaded the nobles of the country to overlook the little boy. Then he had himself proclaimed Duke of Milan, and Beatrice was happy.

This violence and change didn't bother Leonardo very much. He went on with his experiments and his painting. But now he found himself busier than usual, for Lodovico began doing a good deal of pulling down and rebuilding. He sent Leonardo to his country seat to work there, and the notebooks were filled with Leonardo's thoughts and figurings on the subject of gravity. The painter was fascinated by a new irrigation system which had recently been put in. As he watched the machinery by the house, he came to the conclusion, "The more the force is transferred from wheel to wheel, from lever to lever, from ratchet to ratchet, the more powerful it grows and slower."

From this problem he moved on to hydraulics. He could not quite discover how pressure is distributed on the surface of water, but he did observe that in a pump the pressure on the water affects the force of the water pushed out in a fixed ratio. He began to write a treatise on the motion and measurement of water. Then he went on in his thoughts and realized that there was a connection between the behavior of water and that of air. "As the stone thrown into water forms various circles," he wrote, "so a sound spreads in circles through the air."

Nowadays we know this, but until Leonardo began observing and thinking, none of the philosophers and scientists had gone that far. He also invented instruments to measure pressure and currents in rivers, to ascertain what effect these might have on river banks.

But this peaceful period couldn't continue. The aftereffects of trickery were piling up on Lodovico il Moro. Louis of Orleans, a French noble who was cousin and heir to Charles VIII, had as strong a claim to Milan as Charles had to Naples. Now he began trying to press this claim, threatening to bring another

French army into Italy. Lodovico decided that he didn't like the French so much after all. He didn't want Charles, still sitting in Naples, to stay there, spreading his influence.

The Moor set to work and organized a lot of powerful allies—the Pope, Maximilian who was emperor of the Holy Roman Empire, the King of Spain, and the Doge of Venice. Together they declared war on Charles VIII. The poor French King was staggered by this treachery. He and his men were cut off from home, trapped in southern Italy, but he fought his way through the barrier and got back to France at last. After all, he had not been away from home much more than a year. He had lost most of his army and all his gains. It had been a terribly expensive crusade.

It was expensive for Lodovico, too, because he had bribed the allies to join him. Besides, Louis of Orleans still threatened to invade Milan, and the Moor had to outfit his troops all over again. One thing after another called for money. He taxed the Milanese until they complained so loudly that he was afraid of a revolt. He had got his way and was the most powerful prince in Italy, but he was beset with new troubles.

These troubles were passed on to his household, and now Leonardo, too, found himself bothered by the war. First of all, his beautiful horse was a victim. Lodovico simply could not afford to spare all that bronze.

Metal was at a premium; and the 150,000 pounds of bronze that had been earmarked for the horse went instead to the cannon maker to be used in weapons.

This was a tremendous blow to Leonardo, but there was nothing he could do about it. And then at almost the same time his pay was stopped. Leonardo had never been paid very regularly, but until then he had received his money once in a while.

Lodovico stopped paying all his dependents. However, he still expected them to go on working for him, and Leonardo remained in the castle. He was supposed to be decorating rooms with wall paintings and frescoes.

For a while Leonardo actually did this, hoping against hope that Lodovico's treasurer would give him some of the money due him. In the meantime, he had nothing with which to buy food, let alone clothes. At last, after asking Lodovico outright and getting no satisfaction, he actually walked out on the job.

Oddly enough, everybody was surprised by this action. The Duke's secretary reported it in a letter to his master: "The painter who has painted our rooms made something of a scene today, and left on account of it."

Now Leonardo was again on his own. He felt himself opposed by a mass of enemies. In the painter's circle there was a lot of jealousy and backbiting. Plenty of people who had envied him his secure, if ill-paid, position at court were now glad to spread malicious rumors about him.

Leonardo determined to make a living out of the inventions that came so readily to his mind. He had great hopes of his needle-sharpening machine; he figured out how much he could make by running it himself at a certain charge per needle. As always happened in these calculations, Leonardo estimated he could make a good comfortable income. But those were estimates on paper. As far as we know, the machine was never made.

Then he turned around and invented a spinning wheel. Thirty years later, somebody invented almost the same thing and this one was actually manufactured. However, there was one gadget on Leonardo's spinning wheel that wasn't re-invented until a hundred and fifty years ago in England.

Leonardo dreamed up many other improvements for the textile trade. They are there in the notebooks, although they never appeared in solid form. And today we use things very like them.

The two industries that kept Milan going were cloth-making and steel-making. Leonardo was fascinated by iron foundries and often thought of methods to improve the way the work was done. He invented rolling machines "for making thin and uniform tin sheets," and others for gun making. Then there were grinding plants for gun barrels and other improvements, which were, again, wonderfully practical and years ahead of anything that was in actual use.

During this time Leonardo observed the effect of friction, and worked out rules of physics for that. He observed that oil or grease reduced the resistance of friction. When he got so far as to think of roller bearings, he wrote, "This device gives circular motion a duration that seems marvellous and miraculous. . . . These are marvels of the mechanical art!"

However, though all this was exciting, it wasn't earning him anything to live on. Lodovico had been trying to get hold of another famous artist to take Leonardo's place. But everyone had heard of the difficult working conditions under a man who never paid, and famous artists fought shy of Milan. You would have expected Leonardo to go away and try his fortune in some other city, since this one had been so unkind, but he was strangely timid in such ways. He was reluctant to make changes unless he was really forced to do so.

When he came from Florence, he *had* felt he had been forced out because nobody there appreciated him and Lorenzo had never given him a position. In Milan, however, he had actually been recognized and was court painter for years. At least, his vanity was fed. So, even though he was angry with Lodovico, he didn't break off relations altogether.

Finally, his need and the knowledge of Lodovico's need brought him to eat humble pie. He had been the one to walk out; now he was the one to ask to be re-established. He wrote to the Duke, reminding him of his work and suggesting that they have another try. Lodovico assented, and so Leonardo came back into his employ with a new commission to take the place of the poor, abandoned bronze horse. This was to be a large wall painting of "The Last Supper."

This is now Leonardo's most famous work. Art students always hear about it early in their studies—how it was painted right on the wall, and in time was nearly destroyed by paint flaking off, and so on. There is no doubt it was one of Leonardo's most carefully prepared pieces of work. His papers are full of preliminary sketches, and the writings of his friends mention the various problems he encountered. The whole world of art watched while it was being done. Once again Lodovico and Beatrice must have felt very proud of their errant court painter.

The painting was done in the monastery of Lodovico's favorite church near the castle, called Santa Maria delle Grazie. Lodovico decided to have the painting made on one side of the monks' refectory.

In his notebook Leonardo wrote down the ways by which he meant to distinguish the apostles: "One who was drinking has set down his glass and turned his head toward the speaker. Another, twisting the fingers of his two hands and with brows knitted, turns to his neighbor; this neighbor spreads his hands and shows their palms, raises his shoulders to his ears, and opens his mouth in amazement. Another whispers into his neighbor's ear; the listener turns towards him to lend an ear, holding a knife in one hand and in the other the bread half cut through; another, who has turned, holding a knife in his hand, upsets with his hand a glass on the table." And so on, through all the apostles.

This work really captured Leonardo's attention. He went at it with all his mental might. He moved into a small room because he said he could concentrate better there. He thought every evening about what he had done during the day, and in the morning as soon as he woke up he was thinking of it again. When he was hard at work, he forgot to eat, and went on at top speed for days on end. Then he would stop short, and go out every day, anywhere, away from the refectory, wandering about, watching the light on the countryside, still thinking of the picture.

For each face he took great care to find exactly the right model. One day the prior, perhaps made nervous by Leonardo's reputation for being slow, complained to Lodovico that he didn't think the painting was getting on fast enough. Leonardo still hadn't put in Judas or Christ, he said. Now, for once in his life when he heard this complaint Leonardo had a right to feel that this was unfair. He really had gone on quickly with "The Last Supper," compared to his usual speed. He retorted, "What do monks know about painting? Can they paint? It's true that I haven't been to the monastery for a long time. Yet not a day passes without my devoting at least two hours to the work."

Lodovico asked him to explain.

"Why," said Leonardo, "as your Excellency knows, Judas is missing. I can't find a model fit for such an abandoned character. For more than a year I have been going down to the criminal quarter every day where the scum of humanity is to be found, but I haven't yet found what I want. If I can't find it there, I shall have to use the prior's head; it would serve well for the purpose. I've only hesitated to do it out of consideration for his feelings." This made Lodovico roar with laughter.

In time the painting caused as much excitement as the model for the statue of Francesco on horseback. Again Leonardo da Vinci was talked about and praised and imitated. Many people asked him to give lectures about his methods; students clamored to enter his studio. At last he determined to write a book in which he could put all his knowledge, with his theories of how a painter ought to feel, and how people ought to feel about paintings, and what he thought about it compared to sculpture, and so on. He wrote the book and called it a *Treatise on Painting*.

Just at this time the wife of Lodovico died. Beatrice had always been a wild girl, hungry for pleasure, riding madly after the hunt or dancing for hours on end. That winter she injured herself, fell ill and quickly died. Lodovico was grief-stricken for a little while; and he had Leonardo design a little mourning room in her memory, all in black. Before it was finished, the changeable man was feeling better again, and he switched his court painter to another job decorating the great banquet hall next door. Soon Lodovico made plans to marry again. But Charles VIII had his revenge in that matter. He persuaded the girl Lodovico had his eye on to reject her suitor. Charles himself died in 1498.

This death mattered more to Lodovico than did his disappointment regarding marriage. For now Louis of Orleans became King of France, and would soon be able to march on Milan. Lodovico began to get frightened. He rushed around trying to rally his friends to help him defend the state. But after a lifetime of trickery, he found he had no friends. It was common knowledge that he was in grave danger. His flatterers dropped off.

Now Lodovico thought about his sins more seriously than he had done during his short period of mourning for Beatrice. One of the things that plagued his conscience, and which might well have occurred to him before, was his shabby treatment of Leonardo. He made belated amends. Suddenly he presented the painter with a vineyard. There, he said, Leonardo could build a house and settle down near him.

It seems a very odd present to have made when at any moment the enemy might come and drive both the Duke and the painter from the country. But, as usual, Leonardo was too much wrapped up in his experiments to give much thought to the future. He was delighted with the gift. It was the first land he had ever owned. Immediately he plunged into the study of viniculture and wine, and started to plan his house.

Four or five months later, in July, 1499, the French marched into Italy again, under Louis. News arrived in Milan that they were already in Lombardy. Even so, Leonardo didn't worry. After all he wasn't Lodovico, or even an ordinary rich Milanese. He went right on with the work he had in hand, installing a new bathroom for Isabella of Aragon and working out the right temperature of the water, which he planned should be ready mixed, hot and cold, in just the proper proportions. He also continued work on his new treatise, "Motion and Weight."

On the fifth of August, the city gates were opened to the French. Lodovico had learned that a severe ruler who had been tricky and unjust cannot depend on anybody at all in his hour of need. There was no defense. The castle, which should have withstood months of siege, fell to the invaders through the treachery of one of Lodovico's most trusted men. The Moor had to run away.

For Leonardo the worst thing about the occupation was that the Gascon archers in the French army, in wanton sport, practiced their marksmanship on his great clay horse and helped the wind and rain to batter it to pieces. It must have broken his heart to see this gallant effort finally destroyed, even though he had long since given up hope of ever casting it in metal.

Yet he could not have been left very long with a sense that the French were his enemies, for the king, Louis XII, had great admiration for his work. Louis had already heard of Leonardo, of course. Soon after the triumphal entry he went to the monastery of Santa Maria delle Grazie to see "The Last Supper." He even asked if, by any possibility, it could be cut from the wall and carried back to France for his pal-

Archers practiced their marksmanship on the clay horse.

ace. This was quite impossible because the picture was painted on the plaster itself. But later Louis invited Leonardo to work for him. The offer was a flattering one. Leonardo's hungry soul had been almost satisfied. He was more sure of himself. He had "arrived" in spite of Lodovico's stingy treatment for so many long years.

Milan had months of uncertainty after the conquest. The French soldiers quartered on the town were brutal sometimes and stupid. Before long the Milanese regretted that they had welcomed the invaders. In memory, Lodovico did not seem so bad after all.

For this reason they were glad when Lodovico fought his way back to the throne. That is to say, Swiss mercenaries fought the way back for him. The Swiss were excellent soldiers, but after Lodovico had been back in power for a short time they were bought over by the French, and the Duke was out again. This time it was the end for him. He was taken prisoner and carried off to France. There he was to languish in prison for ten years before his death.

Leonardo was not deeply involved in these upsets. He didn't accept Louis's invitation. Probably it seemed like too much of a change for the quiet man. But for a little while he worked for Louis's representative, or viceroy. All the while he hung on to his vineyard.

When the situation continued uncertain, Leonardo decided to move on for a little while to Mantua. Mantua, not far from Milan, was governed by the margrave Francesco Gonzaga and his wife Isabella d'Este, sister of the late Beatrice. Isabella was famous for her interest in the arts. For a long time she had begged Leonardo to do her the honor of coming to stay, and at last he accepted. He set forth with his naughty little servant Giacomo, nicknamed "Salai," which means "the bad one." He had left Milan when he heard that Lodovico had been taken prisoner.

"The Duke has lost his state and his possessions and his liberty, and has brought none of his works to completion," wrote Leonardo calmly. No doubt he reflected that though he himself had failed to make that bronze horse, other people were even worse off.

Isabella d'Este

Chapter 6

THE REIGN OF THE PRINCE

Isabella d'Este, the Margravine of Mantua, was famous in her lifetime. She has continued to be remembered, not for what she did herself, but because of her circle. There are some people who can't paint particularly well, or write, or play music, or compose it, but who nevertheless love the arts. So they surround themselves with persons who can do one or another of these things very well indeed. Isabella's special talent was to surround herself with such people.

Her rank was not very high; her sister Beatrice as a duchess had been much grander. Nor was she rich. She and her husband Francesco Gonzaga had a hard time keeping up appearances to match their title, so she couldn't tempt famous men with promises of fortune. She could not be a patron on the scale of Lorenzo de Medici or Lodovico Sforza, her brother-in-law. Nevertheless she did very well at collecting art and artists. In fact, she did better than a lot of wealthy patrons. This was because she tried hard and kept working at it.

Isabella d'Este took pride in owning a few exquisite pictures and the best statues money could buy—not many, but one or two. She believed she knew a good deal about painting, sculpture and building. It was not beyond her to tell her artist guests exactly how they ought to go about their work. Most of them meekly took it. She encouraged promising young poets, and they wrote songs glorifying Isabella d'Este and told her that her own poems were wonderful. More than others of the nobility, she appreciated Leonardo's talents and was proud of knowing him. She considered him a friend and not just a painter.

When he consented in his offhand way to come to stay at Mantua after he left Milan, she was delighted. At the back of her mind was the hope that she could persuade him to paint a portrait of herself. Isabella never had any scruples about getting what she wanted in the way of pictures.

She had one little trick especially; she would pay a poor artist a small sum in advance, acting as if it were really just a gift to help him along. Then, when she was sure he had spent it, she would begin to remind him that he owed her some work. Politely she would keep reminding and reminding him, until the most dilatory painter would in desperation give her what she was after.

Anyone would, that is, except Leonardo. Here the determined woman met her match. You could go on bothering Leonardo forever and ever; but if he happened to be interested in something other than painting, as he usually was, he would not do your picture, and Isabella found this out.

It was not that Leonardo meant to be ungenerous or tantalizing. He probably had every intention of doing as she wished, at first. He went so far as to make the preliminary sketch of Isabella. She would have been happy to have had that, at least, though it wasn't flattering in the way ladies of the time were used to having their portraits painted. It made her look handsome, as indeed she was, but it also looked rather hard and cold. Her husband hated the picture, just as husbands today sometimes hate photographs of their wives which they think don't do justice to the subject.

One day when Isabella was not looking, long after Leonardo had given up the project and gone to Venice, Francesco gave away her copy of the sketch. So poor Isabella got nothing after all. She kept on writing to Leonardo, and sending him messages, and begging for some painting, any painting, the smallest possible painting. But he never let her have one. In spite of everything, he really didn't seem to like Isabella d'Este.

From Mantua Leonardo went to Venice, the lovely city with canals instead of streets flowing between lacy palaces. Leonardo had a good reason for going to this wealthy city, over and above the fact that he had never seen it before. One of the things that was becoming stronger in his nature was the desire to achieve something with his knowledge of science.

It is not very odd that this genius of a painter should have thought his painting comparatively unimportant. He was much more interested in his studies of physics and chemistry and physiology. Many people are like that, especially those who are always trying to learn more, like Leonardo. The thing they know they can do well is not so interesting to them as the thing they have not yet mastered. That is why Leonardo painted only when he was driven to it by financial needs.

Once in a long while, when he was embarked on a painting like "The Last Supper" that needed a lot of thought and planning, he would be absorbed in it. But it was rather difficult to get him so caught up in a picture that he would finish it as he did that one. And at this time, Leonardo wanted above all to put some of his engineering theories into practice.

It was the turn of the century, the year 1500. Venice found herself in danger from the Turks. They had advanced much farther than anyone in Italy had ever expected; they had even come across the Mediterranean and fought on Italian soil. The Venetians were in a panic. Leonardo is said to have arrived with an introduction from the French noble, Count de Ligny. The Count was ruling Milan as Louis's Viceroy. Leonardo prized this introduction more than anything because it presented him as a *military engineer,* not merely a painter of holy scenes.

Everybody was in such a state of nerves that the newcomer got right to work with his plans for defense. He saw that the river Isonzo could of itself serve as a barrier to the invaders. This was important because the Venetians thought they would not have time to build regular fortresses before the Turks arrived. "A few men, with the aid of such a river, are equivalent to a large number," said Leonardo. He planned sluices to drain off the city's water-highways in case they flooded.

When the authorities complained that it would cost too much, he reminded them that they often spent far more than he needed on unnecessary wars with practically half Europe—"the Empire, the Church, the King of Spain, and the King of France." After that he had no more of such complaints. He also made guns for the Venetians. But most interesting of his preparations for defense was a new invention he thought up. This was to get under the enemy's ships whenever they should approach the city, and bore holes in the bottoms.

Long ago he had got the idea of diving suits from watching divers who carried air bags down under water with them. Leonardo took the idea further and invented watertight suits. These had glass over the eyes so that the wearers could look around, and pipes that carried air from the surface. He also thought of a kind of spear with which the diver could defend himself from dangerous fish, and gloves with webbing between the fingers like duck's feet, to help in swimming. It all suggests the skin-diving outfits that we see in use today.

Leonardo also made up a more elaborate apparatus —a dress with stiff loops to hold off the water's pressure when the diver got in deep. With this he proposed a mask connected with a great bladder of air. This would be emptied when the diver first got in (carrying weights to take him to the sea bottom). Then it would be refilled under water, from other bladders. All these gadgets were to be kept invisible on the surface of the water, so that the enemy might not see them.

Leonardo decided this information should be kept secret. Suddenly he realized that he was actually mixed up in a war. In his notebook he carried a deadly secret that might cause the death of hundreds of people if it got into the wrong hands. For the first time, he seems to have felt twinges of conscience. Until then, the machines he invented for killing men had all been merely so many experiments and theories. Now he had doubts.

Nevertheless, like so many scientists since, he felt it was excusable to use these things when you were on the right side, so he went on inventing them. He thought up "a ship to sink another ship." This was a little craft covered with iron that was to be propelled under water close to the enemy ship to sink it. In other words, he invented a submarine. This he kept secret, too.

What happened to all his inventions remains unknown. History doesn't mention that they were ever used, only that Venice wasn't conquered this time. Was Leonardo bitterly disappointed again? Or was he relieved that the engines of destruction were not to be on his conscience? He left nothing about it in his notes. At any rate he could comfort himself with the thought that at last he had been taken seriously as an engineer.

After Venice Leonardo da Vinci carried out his earlier intention, which had been postponed because of the emergency, and went home to Florence. It was the spring of 1500, sixteen years since he had left the city in anger. The men who had been his comrades and fellow-pupils in youth were anxious to see if he had changed, now that he was forty-eight. (In those days, forty-eight was quite an age.) They observed that he was as strong as ever. Leonardo had always been unusually strong; it was said he could bend a bar of iron with his bare hands.

However, he looked much older, though he had not begun to stoop. He wore glasses, his face was somewhat wrinkled, and his hair was thinner. He looked just a little forbidding. He dressed very carefully and rather richly, his friends reported, but he wouldn't go to the extremes demanded by fashion. In his writings he said, scornfully, that Florentine fops were wearing clothes so long they had to carry them as ladies carry their trains. Quite sensibly Leonardo wore his coats only down to the knee.

His friends were delighted to have him back in Florence. But his family was not particularly interested. Ser Piero was about sixty-five or more, and that really *was* old in the sixteenth century. After his third wife died, he had married again and he had five children by the fourth wife. By this time he had lost interest in his eldest son. He and Leonardo were on reasonably friendly terms, but that was as far as it went.

The first work Leonardo undertook to do in Florence was another painting, an altarpiece in a monastery. He moved outright to the monastery with Salai. But hardly had he settled down when he was overtaken by his old bad habit of getting interested in something outside the commissioned work. I say "bad habit" because there is no doubt it was very vexing to the poor monks who had commissioned the painting.

This time Leonardo's great outside interest was geometry. We cannot really regret that he should have concentrated on geometry, or whatever attracted his brilliant mind. He simply had to go the way his intellect led him, and in fact his studies of geometry did have their effect on his painting. Many of his group paintings were geometrical. The design he finally worked out for the monks in a picture that still exists, "The Virgin and Saint Anne," forms a perfect triangle. When the preliminary drawing, called a cartoon, was finished the monks were so amazed and delighted that they forgot all their complaints.

Word of this new wonder reached the eager ears of Isabella d'Este, and she sent a friend as messenger to beg Leonardo to remember her portrait. Or if he could not bring himself to do that, she wanted some other painting—a Madonna at least.

The messenger wrote to her from Florence that Leonardo seemed to be leading a very unsettled life. He was sick of painting, spent all his time on geometry, and let his assistants do his painting for him. At last this man got to Leonardo himself and carried Isabella's pleading message. But Leonardo put him off. He said that whatever he did at the moment would have to go to the King of France, as he owed him first consideration. If he ever had anything extra, Isabella should get it. This was not strictly true. Leonardo had not committed himself to Louis XII; he only kept the King in mind as someone he might one day depend on. But the excuse served to put off Isabella.

His next patron was not French at all. Instead, Leonardo found himself working for one of the most interesting and wicked figures of the Renaissance—the notorious Cesare Borgia, a Roman-born Spaniard.

Cesare was brought up to be a cardinal, but he hated the limitations of life in the Church and left it. From that time on he plotted and schemed to become the wealthiest and most powerful man in Italy. He was a man so eaten by ambition that no other emotion filled his heart. He had no conscience and no real love or friendship for anyone, though he could assume charm when he liked, and had managed to attract some very pleasant people.

Cesare had spent some time at the court of Louis XII. There he had married a French princess. King Louis was very fond of him, and Cesare's wife loved him.

Yet it was strongly suspected in Rome that Cesare had murdered his own elder brother out of hatred and jealousy. It was more than suspected, it was known, that he never stopped at the murder of other people if they stood in the way of his slightest desire.

In a world where selfishness and violence were commonplace, Cesare Borgia's name was so bad that when he was killed, he was buried just where he fell, in unconsecrated ground. And ever since that day the country people there have sworn that his ghost haunts the neighborhood. Only in our time, in 1954, have his bones been dug up during modern building operations, and at last buried in a nearby churchyard. Cesare Borgia has been remembered and feared for more than four centuries.

This strange creature was handsome and dashing, and was always dressed with great extravagance. He fascinated a Florentine named Macchiavelli to such an extent that Macchiavelli wrote a book, or treatise about him. This he called *The Prince,* describing his idea of what a perfect ruler should be. His model for this perfection was the murderous Cesare.

The Borgia must have had a lot of personal charm, to attract not only the King of France and the secretary and countless others, but also the usually indifferent Leonardo. Cesare wanted Leonardo as one of his court, not so much because he himself was fond of painting, but because he had seen how other important people admired the artist. He tempted Leonardo by asking him to be his architect and military engineer. Leonardo much preferred such work to painting altarpieces for monks, and he accepted willingly.

In 1502, when Leonardo joined him, Cesare had embarked on a series of conquests, intending to carve out for himself a kingdom. He had taken the Romagna by force of arms, and the town of Piombino on the west coast of Italy, which was surrounded by marshes. Leonardo went to Piombino and set to work, as Cesare directed him, figuring out a way to drain the marshy country. Though nobody then knew that mosquitoes carry malaria, it had been observed that fevers seemed to hang over wet ground.

Then Cesare summoned Leonardo to the city of Arezzo, near Florence. A famous mercenary captain, or *condottiere,* Vitellozzo Vitelli, was encamped there. Arezzo under Vitellozzo was in revolt against Florence on its own account, which is the reason Cesare had allied himself with the mercenary. The fact that they were opposing his own city did not deter Leonardo from helping them with his inventions. Clearly Leonardo felt no special loyalty to Florence. After all, the governing body, or Signoria, was not that under which he had had his training; the Medici family he knew had long since been driven out. Most Italians felt loyalty to a ruling family, but the conception of loyalty to a state or nation had not yet entered their heads.

When Cesare and Vitellozzo threatened Florence from the outskirts, the Duke of Milan and the King of France sent troops to assist the Florentines. Cesare then turned his attention to a new conquest, the Duchy of Urbino.

So Leonardo went to Urbino, too, and studied the architecture there. He traveled on, wherever Cesare went, and he never mentions having been shocked by the methods with which the adventurer made his gains. He rarely mentions such matters at all, even as a spectator. It was enough for him to wander about as he did, doing what was asked of him, making his sketches and jotting down observations.

While all this fighting was going on, whispers began to run through Italy that Cesare could not survive much longer. Everyone was complaining, and the King of France was on his way to Milan to see for himself what was happening in Italy. Surely, said the angry Italians, he would not allow this dangerous mad dog of a fellow to continue to run riot!

What they had not counted on was that Cesare was clever enough to appeal to the King's greed. Whenever he was with Louis, he talked of the claim to Naples of the French royal house. Louis insisted that this claim still held good, though Charles VIII had been tricked into abandoning the kingdom after winning it once, in Lodovico's day. In the late summer of 1502, Cesare hurried to Milan to meet Louis, and there the eager onlookers were staggered and disappointed to see that his power of fascination still served him well. Louis seemed to think nothing bad could be true of this plausible, good-looking young aristocrat.

Dizzy with triumph and more than ever sure of himself, Cesare then gave his military engineer full powers to go ahead with tremendous improvements. In the credentials he bestowed on Leonardo he called him "the most excellent and beloved servant, Architect and Engineer General Leonardo da Vinci." The engineer could go where he liked without paying passage; he was to have all the workmen he needed and all the help he asked for. It is no wonder Leonardo didn't see fit to criticize the behavior of Cesare. To his knowledge, no one else had ever been given more power to do the sort of thing he had always longed to do.

So many plans and glittering pictures occurred to Cesare that it was hard to decide what needed his attention first, but he had an idea. The port of Cesena, in Romagna, was a vital spot in the development of his new possessions, but it was rapidly silting up and becoming useless. Leonardo suggested that a canal could be built between the city and the port, and he set to work on it immediately, staying a long time at Cesena.

While he was happily at work on his canal, the people who had been tricked or driven out of their homes by Cesare decided to band together. They made war on him in this fashion and had some success immediately. The Duke of Urbino won back his domain, and Cesare's conquered territory kept shrinking until he was in a state of siege at Imola.

Now one of his strongest enemies was Vitellozzo, whom he had abandoned. Much as they hated Cesare, the Signoria of Florence were more afraid of Vitellozzo. They must make some sort of compact with Cesare. So they sent their secretary, Macchiavelli, to talk matters over with him at Imola. Leonardo, too, was there.

The painter stayed on with Cesare through the winter, while the crafty man spun his webs and intrigues and at last succeeded in persuading Vitellozzo to make friends with him again. It was extraordinary how such a wicked man managed, over and over, to fool people who should have known better.

Before he came to an end of all his crimes, Cesare committed a dreadful one there at Imola. He invited to a great banquet Vitellozzo and another mercenary with whom he was now supposed to be on the best

Cesare ordered them to a back room where they were killed.

of terms. They came, and Cesare promptly led them away from their soldiers into a back room where they were assassinated. Not long afterwards Cesare met his death.

But before that Leonardo had left Imola, and the strange court of Cesare Borgia broke up. In January, 1503, the painter returned to Florence. No one held it against him that he had been working for Cesare. Calm as ever, untouched by the violence and bloody crimes that had gone on around him, Leonardo continued his studies. He was now passionately interested in discovering the secret of flying.

FLYING MACHINES, CANALS AND MEN

Of all the studies that fascinated Leonardo, the one he came back to most frequently was the problem of flying. His earliest memory about flying was a strange one. Very possibly it was a childhood dream, but it was so vivid that he spoke of it later as if it had really happened. It seemed to him that one day he was lying in his little cradle out in the family garden. He was probably between two and three years old. Suddenly a great bird, a kite or hawk, swooped down and stood on his breast and beat his lips once or twice with its tail, and then flew away.

Now, this *could* have happened. As we know, some birds live by preying on other animals. Occasionally they carry off young animals. The great bird on Leonardo's cradle may have been investigating this little living creature, and may have decided that it was too heavy to carry away to a mountain aerie. But would Leonardo have remembered the occasion so well if he had been only two years old?

Whether or not the incident really happened, it stayed in his mind. Like everything that had anything to do with flight it interested him deeply. Like the Wright Brothers who lived in America hundreds of years later, Leonardo could not get the subject out of his head. He would work at it for a while, and then go on to something else. But he always came back to the problem.

In this he wasn't alone. Quite a few people were carrying on experiments and trying to make some sort of flying machine.

Leonardo began, as most pioneers in flying naturally do, with trying to imitate birds' wings. He also watched how the sails carried a ship along, and how an eagle could fly even in rarefied air, high up above our atmosphere.

He planned his flying machine in his usual methodical way, first figuring how big the wings must be to carry the weight of a man. But size was not enough; he must allow for motion. His first attempt was rather on the principle of a surfboard. The middle part was a kite-shaped plank on which the flier was to lie, bound to the machine with iron hoops. He could pull the wings with his arms and raise or lower them by working his legs, as if he were riding a bicycle. A tail-shaped rudder to steer with was moved by the flier's head. The wings were made as like a bird's as he could manage, with ribs of wood for the stretching, cloth pulled tight across, and feathers pasted on. Soon he realized that this would not work, and he changed the pattern to that of a bat's wings. That, too, failed.

The next time he tried to make a flying machine he started out on an entirely different tack. This time the man in the machine was to stand upright between things like stilts, and the wings were made to revolve rather like a helicopter. There were two ladders like a bird's legs to take off with. The flier was to draw these up when he was in the air, as landing gear is retracted in the planes of today.

It is clear from his notes that the inventor wanted

He watched each bird closely as it flew from its cage.

to try out the apparatus from the roof of the Milanese castle where he was working, hidden from all eyes. While figuring out how to keep himself from harm if the machine didn't work, he discovered a very useful gadget. "If a man have a tent roof of caulked linen 12 ells broad and 12 ells high," he wrote, "he will be able to let himself fall from any great height without danger to himself." That, of course, was the parachute.

This earlier research was made during his stay in Milan before the downfall of Lodovico il Moro. Then either Leonardo grew discouraged with the problem or he allowed it to be crowded out of his mind by other interests for a long time after that. Once when he thought of it again, he made several interesting changes. He supplied a motor to the contraption. But then again he put away the idea for a long time, until 1503.

That year, while he was living in Florence, another scientist invented a flying machine. Rather, he finished inventing one on which, like Leonardo, he had been working for some years. This man announced that he was going to try it out, and a great multitude of people came to watch his demonstration. He took off from the roof of a church, the highest place he could find in the city. For a minute or two the heavy machine actually did hover in the air. Then it crashed, back onto the church roof. It was smashed to pieces and the inventor's leg was broken. Nothing more was heard about that machine, but the experiment started Leonardo thinking again about his own attempts to fly.

For months after that he did nothing in painting or anything else. He just watched birds in flight, and made sketches, and tried experiments. The birds he came across during his rambles were not enough to satisfy him; he wanted to get closer. Sometimes he went to the market where little birds were for sale as pets or for food. He would buy one or two of these and open the cages and let them go, and watch them closely as they flew away. Nobody could understand what in the world he was doing.

By this time Florence was at war with Pisa. Belatedly the city rulers remembered that their own Leonardo da Vinci had a reputation for inventing new weapons. They also recollected that he was a military engineer. So they called him in and asked his advice as to how to vanquish the enemy city. Leonardo produced a simple, very effective idea. Why not cut off Pisa from her water supply?

Pisa is on the Arno River, downstream from Florence. The Arno is Florence's big river that runs straight through the middle of the city. Why not go to a point between the cities, dig canals, and simply divert the whole river along a shorter way to the sea at Leghorn? Without water, Pisa would be left quite helpless.

The authorities promptly sent Leonardo out on a survey, to see if the idea was really feasible. Every expert who was consulted agreed that it was. Soon the whole project was actually under way. Leonardo's friend Macchiavelli went back and forth from the scene of the work to the city, arranging the amount of wages for the workmen and so on.

Leonardo wasn't the sort of man who invents something and then turns it over to someone else for the actual working. Instead, he went to the site of the canal-digging and lived there, and spent days in the country, superintending. He was interested in all the details, and was never satisfied with the traditional method of doing a job if he could think of a way to save labor and accomplish the task more efficiently. He invented a treadmill to dredge up earth out of the canal, with buckets on a rotating wheel.

He also designed a lift that could be worked with a crane. The lift was lowered by the weight of an ox that was walked into it. At the same time the weight raised a case of stones or earth at the other end of the rope. Then the ox was led out of the counter-balance and the lift rose again. Three and a half centuries later the same arrangement was invented again by a French engineer.

The canal was getting along well, but after a few months the work was abandoned because its reason for being suddenly disappeared. Florence didn't have to destroy Pisa, after all. The chief people behind the original quarrel died, and the Signoria were glad to drop the idea of war on Pisa.

Leonardo might have found himself out of a job, but instead, his mind went off in a new direction. He had been interested in the canal as a problem rather than a hostile measure. Now that peace had come back to his city he thought that all his work might as well be put to use in a constructive way. He reasoned that if they knew now how to build canals, why not build one for peaceful use?

The Arno could be regulated above Florence instead of below. A canal could be dug and led through three towns where the local industries would benefit. Wool weavers, corn millers, silk spinners, ribbon weavers, blacksmiths, lumber mills, paper mills—all industries would be worked by water power. Everyone would be better off.

Leonardo was able to convince the Signoria that such a gigantic effort would be profitable. Work on the canal was begun. But now he found himself in the familiar situation of needing money to keep his little household going. As usual, he turned for payment to the one talent which never failed him as long as he didn't fail it—painting.

The Signoria, to commemorate this happy year when everything seemed to be turning out for the best, wanted a series of frescoes painted on the ceiling of their council chamber. Leonardo suggested himself for the commission, and the Signoria agreed. They told him what they had in mind as a subject for the paintings. It was the story of the Battle of Anghiari in 1440, when the Florentines had defeated the Milanese.

Leonardo threw himself into the work with the same sudden gusto that he had shown when he painted "The Last Supper." He was attracted by the new type of subject. The man who had made his name with tranquil pictures of the Virgin and Child now spent all his time thinking of scenes of violence: of rearing, fighting horses and snarling warriors and blood-soaked battlefields.

For a long time in his preliminary sketches Leonardo practiced drawing horses in battle, and then he turned his attention to roaring human faces. He drew angry men screaming, and horses with their lips wrinkled back and their faces furious as no horses have ever looked in life. Finally it was hard to tell whether he was drawing horse or human being. The final cartoon, a writhing mass of horses and men mixed up in a close fight, was planned so that it would fit in a natural manner over the windows of the council chamber. Leonardo used the windows as if they were bridges in his landscape.

But all this preparation took time. The Signoria waited and waited. In 1504, they put pressure on Leonardo, just as other clients had done in the past, fearing that otherwise they would never get their frescoes. They reminded him that they had already paid something in advance and they must have the cartoon before another year had passed. This warning did not send Leonardo rushing back to his studio, because he was so deeply absorbed in the work of the canal, and the theories that arose from it. Now Leonardo was fascinated by water. He was finishing his treatise on it.

From water he returned to his other old love, light. From there he went on with his bigger questionings. What was the nature of the earth? What were the relations of air, fire and water to the planet? Was the moon surrounded, too, by these elements? Was the sun a planet, and did it really move around the earth as it was believed to do?

You can see that all these questions called for a lot of careful thought, and it is no wonder that Leonardo didn't get on faster with the Battle of Anghiari. Instead, he invented a telescope.

In July, 1504, that tough old man Ser Piero da Vinci died at the age of seventy-seven. Leonardo does not seem to have given way to any grief for his father. He put the fact down in his notebook, adding that his father had left ten sons and two daughters. Perhaps he did feel some sensations of regret. But if so he didn't mention them, and it wasn't like him to write such things down anyway.

When Ser Piero's will was read, Leonardo discovered that his father had been just as indifferent toward his eldest son as the son had been toward him. Perhaps Piero forgot Leonardo altogether, or perhaps he just assumed that Leonardo was so famous and rich that he wouldn't need any of his father's money. Whatever the reason, Ser Piero had left his money to be divided up among the other eleven children. He didn't mention Leonardo. Even with that, the brothers and sisters weren't satisfied. Soon they began to quarrel among themselves and try to take more than their share. They went to law about it.

Ser Piero had a brother, Francesco, who had lived in the Vinci house and had always been especially fond of Leonardo. He was indignant about the will. To show how he felt he immediately made his own will, naming Leonardo his sole heir. Leonardo was to be very glad to get that money when Francesco died. For in spite of his fame, he was always hard up. His accounts show that he was trying to live as economically as he possibly could, with only the old serving-woman to look after him.

While the younger Vinci children were going to court and fighting over the estate, Leonardo refused to argue about the share he should have had. But Uncle Francesco and his other friends kept pushing him and telling him he should contest the will. In the end he did make a claim, and seems to have got something out of it. It took years, however.

At the time of his father's death, Leonardo was

again in trouble, because the canal project did not go well after all. It was all right for a while, and the river flowed just the way it was supposed to, in the new channel that had been dug. But then in hot weather the Arno dried up, as it does sometimes, and when it started to flow again it went back into its old bed. Some officials said it would be too costly to work on the system and correct it; others insisted that the work should be done. After a long squabble the workmen returned to the site. Everything was almost ready and the people on Leonardo's side, especially Macchiavelli, heaved a great sigh of relief.

Then came the autumn rains, much worse than usual. The canal overflowed, and some ships that had taken refuge in the artificial basin near the sea were wrecked and eighty sailors drowned. Public opinion turned violently against the canal. The people of Pisa took matters in their own hands and filled it up again. Everybody made fun of the Florentines and, of course, they laughed at Leonardo most of all.

Leonardo simply went back to his frescoes. Usually when things went wrong with his non-painting activities, his work in painting was enough to help him forget the blow his vanity had received. No matter how much it failed to satisfy his ambition, it *was* the thing the world believed he did better than practically anybody else. Though Leonardo neglected painting whenever he got a chance, he realized what he owed to this magnificent talent. With it he won the acclaim his spirit needed. But even here in his own world, something now happened to distress him.

Among artists, as among any other group of men, fashions rise and fade. Leonardo's work was so well accepted that he seemed to be above the laws of change. But beneath him there were always struggles and heartbreaks and accusations among the other artists. Lately Florence had been electrified by the sudden appearance of a young man named Michelangelo Buonarroti, who carved and painted figures in a new way.

Michelangelo concentrated on muscular development; his men always looked as if every muscle in their bodies was working. He had a violence and a force that had not been seen before in the work of the Florentines, who had always aimed at quiet, religious sweetness.

The other artists had different feelings about this new style. Some welcomed it as an exciting change, and others were rather shocked. But they all knew that they were face to face with an important development. The public went wild over Michelangelo's new statue, the famous "David." They called it "The Giant."

When "David" was put on exhibition, everybody

came to see it, including Leonardo. It never occurred to him to be jealous, though many of his colleagues were. It interested him, as all new things did. He studied it and made a sketch of it in his notebook, and when the committee appealed to him on a dispute concerning the statue, he gave his opinion without prejudice.

The dispute was this: Should the marble "David" be placed out of doors before the Palace of the Signoria? This was the place of greatest honor that could be granted any statue in Florence. But marble does not last forever in the sun and the rain. Or should it be put into the Loggia dei Lanzi where it would be sheltered under a roof, but not so much in the public eye? Many artists would have liked to get it out of the way as much as possible.

While the argument went on, feeling ran so high about the statue that Michelangelo's friends had to stand guard over it at night, to keep it from being damaged. Unknown people had been throwing stones at the swathed figure, and though nobody ever proved it, Michelangelo was probably right in suspecting that this was the deed of angry rivals.

Michelangelo was a quick-tempered young man with a suspicious nature. His sudden success, with its attendant criticism, had made him even harder to get along with. He thought everybody was against him.

And like most very young artists he was contemptuous of the older ones.

The argument about where his statue was to be put made him wild with rage. He wanted it in the most prominent place, in the open before the palace, and never mind the wind and the rain.

The Florentines went on and on, talking about it and taking a poll of different artists' opinions. When they asked Leonardo where he thought it should go, he agreed with another artist who had been very fair and sensible in his statement. The other man said that he thought "David" would be better protected in the Loggia, and Leonardo agreed. Michelangelo immediately made up his mind that Leonardo was against him, like all the others.

In the end, it was decided that Michelangelo himself should choose the site, and he cast his vote without hesitation for the open square. So it was done. But the young sculptor had got the idea firmly fixed in his head that this great man Leonardo—this spoiled, petted, proud old man (Leonardo was fifty)—was an enemy. He had a lot of enemies, he thought, and Leonardo was the worst. In the days that followed, Michelangelo quarreled with many other colleagues. Then at last came the time when he was able to let fly at Leonardo, who made him angriest of all.

Many Florentines used to sit around talking about

philosophy, playing games with ideas and words in pleasant fashion, and discussing the classics. One day when a group of them were indulging in this pastime, they saw Leonardo walk past. They hailed him and asked him to come and settle some point for them. It was a game in which he excelled. This question had something to do with Dante. Leonardo knew that Michelangelo was fond of the poet's works and knew a lot about them, so he gestured toward the younger man and said pleasantly:

"You had better ask Michelangelo; he will expound it to you."

Michelangelo got very angry. Instead of realizing that the remark was courteous, a genuine compliment from an old student to a bright young one, he thought it was a veiled insult. He shouted, "Explain it yourself, you who made a model of a horse to cast in bronze, and then couldn't make the casting and cravenly abandoned the work!"

Everybody was struck dumb. Michelangelo walked off, pausing to shout one more insult, "And those fat Milanese geese trusted a task like that to you!"

Leonardo stood there for a minute, silent, his face flushed. Then he walked away, very straight and quiet.

Chapter 8

HOPE FOLLOWS DISAPPOINTMENT

Michelangelo's cruel snub must have hurt Leonardo, for the bronze horse had been very near his heart. He realized that a man who tries to do great things is bound to encounter great failures from time to time. But it was painful to be reminded of this failure above all others. It was unfair as well. He had never had a chance to cast the horse in bronze, but Michelangelo made it sound as if he had tried to do it and had muddled the task.

The young sculptor seemed to have made up his mind to persecute the older artist. The Signoria of Florence had asked Leonardo to decorate the whole council chamber with frescoes, and his "Battle of Anghiari" took care of only one side of it. But now Michelangelo asked them to let him do the opposite side, and they accepted the offer. It was not surprising that they should have done so, since Leonardo was being so very, very slow. Many a client of his had turned to some other artist in despair, after waiting years for the work to be completed. Still, Leonardo was worried.

Michelangelo promptly set to work on his subject, a group of bathing soldiers whose naked bodies would show off the muscles he painted so well. From the moment he began preparing his cartoon the art students of Florence had a wonderful time. They went back and forth happily from one studio to the other, comparing the work of these two famous masters, talking about them, and arguing as to their special virtues. Not only the students came to watch. It was fun for the whole public of Florence.

Leonardo had signed a promise to have his cartoon

ready by a certain time. For a wonder, he lived up to the agreement. Michelangelo had stirred him up and hurried him. At last Leonardo was ready to put the design on, sketching high up on the wall. First he had a scaffold built on which he could work comfortably. Mural painters always had to do that. Then he began to mix the paints or, rather, directed his assistants in mixing them. The first problem of a man who paints a fresco is to prepare the surface on which he is putting his picture. Just as Leonardo had prepared the wall for "The Last Supper," he had to put something on the plaster or stone of the council-room wall. It was too rough and damp by itself to hold paint. He also had to cover the finished painting with a fixative.

The choice of stuff to be used was always a matter that interested Leonardo's colleagues. Each one had his own ideas. As usual, Leonardo wanted to experiment and try new methods. This time for a fixative he used some preparation that he had read about in an ancient book. First he tried it out on the cartoon and found it satisfactory. The only trouble was that it was awfully slow in drying. Growing impatient, Leonardo thought of a way to hurry up the drying by building a hot fire near it and closing the room up. This worked very well.

Now he started on the important part of the fresco,

outlining the figures and filling them in with paint. It took a long, long time, as his painting always did. But as it neared completion, the Florentines saw that it was going to be worth waiting for. They agreed that it was one of the best things Leonardo had ever done. The struggling group of soldiers and horses, the glowing colors, the arrangement of design which like all his groups was geometrical in shape—never had there been such a fresco! It looked more like inlaid jewels or enamel than paint.

Leonardo, too, felt as though he had achieved something outstandingly good, though usually he was hard to please about his own work. He had been on this for a long time and had thought very hard about it. The subject was not the sort of thing that he was famous for. It was really much more Michelangelo's kind of thing, with all that action and violence. So it was natural that he should feel rather proud of himself. He must have been pleased to show the young man who had been so unkind about his bronze horse that he was still a master.

However, there was one thing about the painting as he brought it to completion that worried him. The fixative stayed wet for a long time. The paint remained sticky. This was a serious matter, for wet paint would attract dust and insects. Later, his critics said that Leonardo was always too fussy. He should have let it alone and waited, they said, and in time it would have dried of itself. But that was not Leonardo's nature. He had dried the cartoon with a hot fire. There was no reason, he thought, why he shouldn't use the same trick with the finished painting.

So, just as he had done before, he had a hot bonfire built up near that part of the wall. He lit it and waited confidently for it to do its work. But this time a terrible thing happened. The paint must have been mixed wrong. As the flames licked up to the horses and the fighting men, the colors began to melt and run down the wall. Before his horrified eyes, all the beautiful work disappeared in an ugly blur of shapeless, blotchy brown.

And there, once more, was a tragic failure for Leonardo. Imagine how he felt! Now Michelangelo would have all the more reason to jeer at him, and the Signoria would complain. Already they were talking about how good Michelangelo's cartoon was. This had been a competition and Leonardo had lost. At least he had lost the first round. And in the mood he was in, he felt he would never have another try at that fresco. He wouldn't have the heart.

During the time he was preparing and painting the "Battle of Anghiari" he was, of course, doing several other things all at once. He was writing a four-volume treatise on the flight of birds. Also he was trying secretly to construct the flying machine to end all other attempts—the flying machine that this time was going to fly properly. Also he was working on a portrait that seems to have interested him more than any he ever did. It has a different history from the others.

It was the portrait of Mona Lisa del Giacondo, the wife of a wealthy merchant. For centuries since, people have wondered why Leonardo should have been so wrapped up in this particular subject. Many ladies of more wealth and beauty and better breeding were turned down when they asked Leonardo to paint their portraits. Yet, according to his notebooks, Leonardo took immense pains with this portrait, and he kept coming back and coming back to it. Sometimes, in order to get the lady to smile in just the manner he wanted, he even hired musicians to come to the house and play while she was sitting, so that she wouldn't get tired of smiling. Why so much trouble just for this one woman?

Of course, some people have thought he must have been in love with her. But his friends didn't think so, and it seems unlikely. In all his life Leonardo never gave any sign of falling in love in a romantic way. He was too much absorbed in the hundreds of things he was studying. There was no gossip about La Gioconda. And a mere love affair would not explain his passionate

Musicians played while he painted the portrait of Mona Lisa.

interest in the picture in any case. Painting and love do not often mix in just that way.

She was a nice-looking woman, but no raving beauty. Nor, according to all accounts, was she particularly intelligent or interesting. She just happened to be the subject of the picture that Leonardo worked on for years. He put everything he had into that painting which is known as the "Mona Lisa."

You must have seen reproductions of it hundreds of

times. Not very long ago it was stolen from the Louvre in Paris, and then later was recovered. Dozens of romantic stories have been written about it. When it goes on exhibition in other places, people get into a line to see it. Probably it is the best-known painting in the world. Critics have written thousands of words about it—the landscape in the background, the "mysterious smile" on the lady's face, and all the rest of it. They have speculated as to what the smile means.

Sooner or later you will be sure to come across Walter Pater's essay on the "Mona Lisa," with the phrase, "and the eyelids are a little weary."

You may wonder what all the fuss is about, as other people have wondered. Another writer says rather coldly that Mona Lisa looks like a landlady at some seaside resort, falsely smirking while she guesses how much she dare ask you for room rent. Most painters will explain that it isn't the subject that matters in a painting anyway, but the way it is done. Certainly it is useless to speculate on what Leonardo thought of La Gioconda herself.

Actually, the famous Mona Lisa smile is very much the same smile that Leonardo painted on several faces in his other portraits. It looks like Leda's smile in "Leda and the Swan," and like St. John the Baptist's in a painting made later on. It is probably silly to talk too much about the painting. To look is one thing, and to listen or read is quite another. For my part, I am glad that Leonardo had this work to comfort him when his "Battle of Anghiari" went wrong, but I don't think "Mona Lisa" is beautiful.

If such an old rumor can be taken seriously, that year marked yet another deep disappointment for Leonardo da Vinci. Because of his desire to keep the matter secret, nobody seems to be certain about his experiment with his new flying machine. But he often wrote about it in his notebook, and drew pictures as he changed his plans.

He was getting so crafty that he didn't call it a flying machine any more. Now it was "the great bird," as if he were jealous of his mystery. The book he planned on the flight of real birds was all a part of his preparation.

But Leonardo didn't stop with birds; he studied bats and insects too—the way their wings were made, and their muscles, and all the different details he could see. He learned that a bird doesn't necessarily keep beating its wings to stay aloft. Often it glides on the air, taking advantage of the wind. As he watched how a bird steers itself, he stumbled on several important mechanical laws.

He saw much more about a bird than anyone else could. "Beginnings of things are often the cause of big results," he wrote. "So in those birds which can support themselves above the course of the winds without beating their wings, a slight movement of wing or tail, serving them to enter either below or above the wind, suffices to prevent their fall." He noted that a bird prevents itself from landing too suddenly by lowering its tail and spreading out the feathers.

It has often been said that angels—or, for that matter, men—couldn't possibly fly with the wings such creatures are represented as having in pictures. A man would need an enormous wingspread to support his weight in air, and the muscles necessary to move such wings would be so disproportionate that he would be a monster. The same objections were being made in Leonardo's day, but he did not agree. He didn't expect to produce genuine wings, of course. But he argued that in a flying machine the wings need not be so big as all that, for a bird had much more muscle than it needed merely for flying, just as a man has more muscle in his legs than he needs merely to stand upright. Leonardo calculated that a man's legs were twice as strong as they need have been. The rest of the strength in both cases was for extra effort. A bird must carry food, or chase small insects and animals, and a man must work and carry heavy weights. For his flying machine Leonardo reckoned that the wings should be about sixty feet across.

All his study of air currents and the behavior of birds in the wind finally brought him around to the principle of the glider. He realized that his flier would be safer high up in the air than low down. Big birds fly high for that reason.

With all these things in mind he now got to work making the great bird. He built the wings on the principle of a bat's wings, using silk ropes and strong cloth and leather. The body of the "bird" was a boat-shaped seat. The flying man was not to be fastened in. Leonardo had now decided that he must be free "from the girdle upwards," so that the center of gravity could shift when necessary. Everything was ready now for the trial flight.

That spring of 1506 Leonardo was taking a holiday in Fiesole, the beautiful suburb of Florence. He resolved to make the trial flight from a mountain near his house there. This mountain, called Swan Mountain, had a steep crest. In his private journal he wrote, "From the mountain that bears the name of the great bird, the famous bird will take its flight and fill the world with its great fame."

On a different page he wrote again, "The great bird will make its first flight—upon the back of its great swan—filling the whole world with amazement, filling all records with its fame, and bringing eternal glory to its birthplace."

There was a rumor that one day some people in Fiesole saw a great bird rise up from Swan Mountain, and then saw it disappear. If Leonardo actually succeeded in gliding for a little, he must have fallen and smashed his machine. And he must certainly have had a miraculous escape; otherwise the world would have heard of his injury. Whatever took place, he said nothing about it, and wrote no more about the great bird in his notebooks. The experiment was yet another failure. A splendid one, but a failure nevertheless.

With these two catastrophes and the enmity of Michelangelo to trouble him, Leonardo decided that he no longer enjoyed living in Florence. He had made a similar decision many years before and had gone to Milan. This time, oddly enough, the same thing was to happen.

Just after the destruction of his fresco, he received an invitation to come to Milan to visit Charles d'Amboise, Sire de Chaumont, the French noble who was now Viceroy of Milan. The chance to enjoy a change of scenery and to look at his property, so long neglected, was not to be missed. Leonardo accepted.

But it was not easy to get away. The Signoria reminded him that he had not yet repaired the ruined fresco in the council room. He had been paid something in advance for the picture. He had made them wait a very long time for it. He had spoiled it once it was made, and now he was proposing to run out. They were angry. One cannot blame them. Yet one cannot pity them either. All along, they should have treated their best painter with greater consideration.

However, the head of the Signoria did not quite dare to prevent Leonardo's going. An invitation from the Sire de Chaumont was nearly the same as a summons from the King of France, who exercised control over a good part of Italy by this time. Leonardo was permitted to leave, but he had to sign an agreement promising to come back within three months. He also had to leave a deposit of a considerable sum of money, practically all he had, which he could not have back unless he called for it in person. Then the Signoria relinquished him, and he hurried straight to Milan.

The Viceroy of Milan was very young, but he had the sense, which no Florentine of importance seemed to have, to appreciate Leonardo da Vinci for the genius he really was. Chaumont made a great fuss over the painter, and insisted that he was honored to be allowed to entertain such a man. What was most delightful for Leonardo was that this young French noble didn't seem to expect him to be just a painter of Madonnas and saints. Chaumont, too, had visions of wonderful cities and great architectural conceptions. He actually wrote to the head of the Florentine Signoria, telling him that this man had not been appreciated for the many-sidedness of his genius.

It was high time the Florentines were told this.

Leonardo would have been happy to remain indefinitely with the man who understood him so well. By the time the three months were up, he was deep in a lot of projects for building palaces and dredging rivers. He had never been so content. To both himself and his patron it seemed impossible that he should go so soon, but when he asked the Signoria for an extension of leave of another three months, the reply was sharp and unpleasant.

"Leonardo da Vinci has not behaved as he should to this Republic; for he has taken a good sum of money and has scarcely more than begun an important work which he was to do."

The letter said a lot of other stern things, and ended, "We desire that there shall be no further requests, since the work is for the satisfaction of the community, and we cannot allow it to be further delayed without failing in our duty."

Chaumont replied politely, with a lot of flattery, repeating his request even more earnestly. Still the Florentines refused. The affair at last had to be settled through the intervention of King Louis XII himself. Chaumont appealed to him.

Louis XII was still in France, but he planned soon

to come to Italy, and he spoke to the Florentine ambassador very plainly on the matter. "It is time for your Signoria to do me a favor," he said, referring to something he had lately done for Florence. "Write to them that I desire to make use of the services of Maestro Leonardo, the painter, who is now in Milan, as I wish to have some works of his; and see to it that the Signoria authorize him to enter my service at once, and to remain at Milan until I arrive there. And write to Florence in such a way that it shall have effect, and do it at once, and let me see the letter."

The Florentine ambassador was very much surprised that the King should make such a fuss merely about one of their local artists. But he wrote the message dutifully to the Signoria, as he had been told to do. In explanation of this strange royal whim he added, "And all this has happened in consequence of a small picture of his which was recently brought here and is regarded as a very admirable work."

Louis XII, too, wrote to the Signoria: ". . . And as soon as you receive these letters, write to him that he is not to move from Milan until our arrival."

Thus the year that had been so disastrous for Leonardo ended happily. He was back in Milan where he had spent sixteen years of his life, back in the very castle where he had served in the past as an ill-paid, neglected court painter. He was in circumstances that he would not have dreamed of earlier. Now he was honored, and princes were quarreling for his services, and he was free to indulge in all the dreams he liked—those reveries that so irritated his fellow Florentines. His kind patron encouraged him in all matters for which, until then, he had been mocked. Leonardo began to love Milan.

Chapter 9

SCIENCE AND ART

Louis XII was vague about the date of his arrival in Italy when he wrote that letter—he only said it to help Chaumont and Leonardo. But as things turned out, he really had to come over the mountains after all. The state of Genoa was supposed to be under

French control, but at this time the Genoese tried to defy the King. So Louis collected a magnificent army, like the one Charles had brought over before him, and went to Genoa.

At the very sight of these thousands of splendid soldiers, all armed to the teeth, the Genoese backed down. There was no battle at all, and the French occupied the city. Then Louis went on to Milan to pay a visit to his viceroy and spend a few months.

He arrived in May, 1507. Naturally his presence set off a whole round of parties and celebrations. It must have seemed like old times to Leonardo, who was called on to furnish special amusements and entertainments just as he had done in the days of Lodovico il Moro. But he enjoyed himself far more at the French court than he had ever done with the Sforza clan. These men understood him and appreciated him and did not keep him on starvation wages as the gross Lodovico had done.

Still, Leonardo was always being reminded of the other time, because a lot of familiar faces appeared at the balls and plays. All the nobility of North Italy had accepted the new state of affairs. It was almost as if the castle had always been occupied by Frenchmen.

One of the guests might well have complained that Leonardo had forgotten all about her, but she didn't.

This was Isabella d'Este, who was thoroughly enjoying the social season. Probably Leonardo groaned when he saw her coming, because she had never stopped sending word to him and begging for that picture.

Now that he was under the wing of the royal house of France he always had an excellent excuse. He was painting something for Louis XII; he was designing a palace for Sire de Chaumont; he was booked up for months, even years, ahead. Isabella could not argue that she was more important than these gentlemen. And in any case she had a lot of new lions to keep her happy.

Within a few months Leonardo realized that he was very popular. This made him happy and sure of himself and his future. He determined to cut himself off from Florence completely by settling the quarrel with the Signoria. So he sent word that the deposit he had left with them and whatever other money he had in the city were to be theirs. This settled the affair of the advance they had paid for the Battle of Anghiari fresco. So now he did not have to go back unless he wanted to. He was free. Never again would he have to work on the fresco that had brought him so much shame and trouble. He had a clear conscience and he was a free man, thanks to the Viceroy of Milan.

Also, he was able to take pupils again, as befitted a master. His personal arrangements were still as simple as ever. The servant, Salai, was always there, a burden Leonardo was years in getting rid of. Usually some old woman did the housekeeping and the real work of looking after him.

When he began to take on apprentices again, he found a genuine helper in the person of Francesco Melzi. Melzi was a very young man, the son of an important Milanese family. He started out wanting to learn to paint just as an accomplishment, not a life work. He had some talent, however, and the better he and Leonardo got to know each other, the more he determined to stay with the painter. Melzi looked after Leonardo much better than the selfish Salai had ever done. He was very loyal and was to be a great comfort in Leonardo's old age, taking the place of a devoted son to the lonely man.

Leonardo had been in Milan nearly a year and a half. He was happy and busy, spending his time on architectural designs and city planning, painting for the King, studying science as he loved to do, and turning his hand now and then to the amusing gadgets that Chaumont wanted for his parties. For one great ball he made one of his blue ceilings that looked like the sky with birds flying around over the heads of the dancers. They were artificial birds on strings hung through the roof.

At this time Leonardo decided that he must go to Florence for a visit. You remember that when his father died he had left nothing to Leonardo in his will. His brother Francesco, to make up for this slight, named Leonardo as his sole heir.

Now Francesco was dead, and Leonardo's greedy younger brothers and sisters were contesting their uncle's will. They insisted that they should have the property, that Leonardo had no right to it. Probably they thought he was too busy in Milan with all his grand acquaintance to put up a fight against them.

But Leonardo was angry. In return for what they were trying to do to him, he started a new claim against his father's will, saying that he had a right to part of *that* inheritance. To do this, he must be in Florence and urge his own case.

Lawsuits in Italy took months and months. If you didn't have powerful backing, they were likely to drag on for longer than that. So Leonardo tried to prepare the way for quick action, as well as success, by taking with him as many letters from very important people as he could gather.

Louis XII himself wrote to the Signoria, saying that "our dear and well-beloved Léonard de Vinci, our painter and engineer in ordinary" was forced to come to Florence because of litigation over certain inheritances. Because he, the King, needed Leonardo back again very soon, he begged the authorities to hurry the matter up "in the best and briefest delivery of justice that may be." That was very useful, and it must have delighted Leonardo to be the King of France's own engineer. He couldn't possibly have asked for a better title. Besides this he brought a letter from Charles d'Amboise, affirming that the King was in a hurry for Leonardo to come back because the artist was working on a special picture for him.

Leonardo had other influential friends too. He got them all to use their names, to ask favors from the people of Florence who might help put the lawsuit through without undue delay. Then he himself went to Florence, not as a man looking for work but rather as a dignitary who was in a hurry. He found the people who could handle the affair and turned over his documents and stated his case, and got things moving as well as he could. But he knew it would be a long business in spite of all this. Legal affairs were never settled right away, even for the great.

He had already arranged to stay with an old friend during the time he must spend in the city. This friend was a younger man, Rustici. He had known of Leonardo a long time, ever since Rustici first started work as an apprentice in Verrocchio's studio some time after Leonardo had finished his own apprenticeship.

Rustici was a professional sculptor and painter like the others. Unlike most of them he also had money of his own and didn't depend on what he could earn. He was not merely a dabbler. He could do good work, and when he had a job he was just as eager as anyone else to do it as well as possible. He had always tried to follow in Leonardo's footsteps.

The two men had a lot in common. Rustici, too, was interested in finding out things about air and water and flying and so forth. Also, like Leonardo, he was not conventional. He liked unusual animals, and filled his house with very odd pets. There was a porcupine running around loose and a tame eagle that flew through the rooms and frightened strangers. A pet raven that could talk was free to fly as it liked. Rustici was the center of a group of young people who enjoyed a fresh outlook and tried to outdo each other in eccentricity.

At the time Leonardo arrived in Florence, his host had just been awarded the most important commission that had ever come his way, and was much excited about it. The city fathers had asked him to make bronze groups to put over the doors of the Baptistery, where the marble figures that had stood there for years had finally crumbled away. Rustici designed huge figures for this purpose.

Making the groups involved a number of technical problems, and he found Leonardo very kind and helpful in solving them. Needless to say, lots of other sculptors of Florence criticized Rustici for getting Leonardo to help, because they were jealous. They said he was "exploiting" his famous guest, but neither Rustici nor Leonardo paid any attention to this ill-natured gossip.

Leonardo enjoyed life at Rustici's house. The young man was a lively person, and so were his friends. They tried to outdo each other in mechanical tricks and practical jokes. They would give dinner parties and command each other to make new toys for the occasion.

One night at Rustici's house when everybody was sitting at the table a tree suddenly grew up through the floor with plates and everything for dinner on its branches, which swung over the table and handed each guest his first course. Then it went back through the floor until time for the next course when it came back with more plates, and so on. It was just the sort of silly, harmless invention that delighted Leonardo.

In this friendly atmosphere he worked constantly, inventing new machines of all sorts. He decided that it was time to rearrange his papers and leave them in some sort of order for posterity. For while he had started so many books and treatises and collections, he never had time to finish any of them. He didn't really want to finish things, when it came to the point. As soon as he thought of bringing something to completion he would decide he didn't know enough about it as yet, and he kept the book open to catch any new thought he might want to pop into it.

However, for the moment he did want to get his books into print, and at Rustici's house he had enough leisure to get started. Characteristically, he drew up his plans for the publishing, and wrote a note to his future readers: "Begun at Florence . . . on the 22nd day of March, 1508. And this is to be a collection without order, taken from many papers which I have copied here, hoping to arrange them later each in its place, according to the subject of which they may treat."

Then, being Leonardo da Vinci, he went off at a tangent, set to work and designed a new kind of printing press which was a great improvement on the one that had been in use for the past century. Soon afterwards, as we would have expected, he decided not to publish his works just yet after all. There was still so much to be added! Instead, he returned to his old interest, anatomy.

The dissection of human bodies was not shocking to the world of Leonardo. Some years before, there had been a lot of prejudice against it, but during the Renaissance when everyone was keen to learn and study, the objectors lost ground. Dissection of the dead was an accepted affair.

Three years before this, after a criminal had been hanged, some famous anatomy professors were permitted to do a public dissection of the body. One of them lectured and pointed out the work to the audience while the others did the actual cutting up. Anybody who wanted to could come and watch. Naturally not many people wanted to, and yet there were quite a few who were interested enough to brave the unpleasantness. As for artists like Leonardo and Michelangelo, the world understood that they must study bodies so that they would know about bones and muscles.

Leonardo had already dissected a number of bodies. Now he set to work to do more. He had an arrangement with various hospitals whereby he was permitted to use the unclaimed bodies of patients soon after they had died. From the careful notes he kept on all this, the doctors of today can often diagnose what it was that killed those patients so many years ago. One old man had obviously been a victim of arteriosclerosis. Another had tuberculosis.

Not everybody would have had Leonardo's nerves, to hold up to this kind of research. There were no refrigerators at that time and nothing was known of preservatives. Often Leonardo had to work all day and all night to finish before the body was buried. In his notebook he warned people that it was a difficult task. "You might be prevented by loathing," he said. But he was tough.

One of the most interesting things he said about all this difficult dissection concerns the importance of illustrating descriptions of anatomy. He said that it was much easier and safer to draw a picture of the thing you were describing than to depend wholly upon words. This is perfectly true. No medical student could learn half so quickly or so well if his textbooks didn't have diagrams to illustrate what is being taught.

Leonardo used many drawings along with words in his anatomical studies. "In order . . . to give a knowledge of the true form of any part of the body of man . . . ," he wrote, "I shall make it a rule to provide four representations, from four sides, of every part. And of the bones I will provide five, by cutting them through the center."

His drawings were so accurate that they could be used for medical textbooks today. As he made these drawings, Leonardo also discovered much about the human body that was not known before he observed it. He drew the spine so that the observer can see how it functions; he figured out how the ribs move

He studied the skeleton and made detailed sketches.

with breathing. He made a remarkable study of the skull. He made twenty anatomical drawings of the hand.

At another time he reported, after exhaustive study, what he had found out about muscles. But it was when he came to the action of the heart that he got close to the discoveries of later centuries. "The heart is a vessel formed by stout muscles, vivified and nourished by arteries and veins, as are also the other muscles." At another time he wrote vividly, "The heart is the nut which gives rise to the tree of the veins."

Many of the laws of nature which he perceived had never been put in anything like the correct light before. We cannot cease to marvel at Leonardo's remarkable powers of observation.

We must remember the great number of things he was doing, all the time. He would not sit down at one subject like anatomy, or physics, or the chemistry of paint, and work at it for years until he had squeezed all the juice out of it. No, he would keep coming back to it as he did with the flying machine, year after year. Then he would break off to study something else such as the nature of water. Yet he was always able to take up a subject where he had left off. With this method, in one lifetime, he rolled up a sum of knowledge that it took the rest of mankind generations to arrive at.

Leonardo planned to do a book about the anatomy of animals, "the movements of animals with four feet; among which is man, who likewise in his infancy crawls on all fours." He dissected a bear and an ape. He intended to show "the extent of the differences between the foot of the bear or ape and the human foot." (A bear's foot, as you may already know, has a very human appearance. It was natural that Leonardo should compare it with an ape's.)

He got the body of a lion that had just died in the city zoo in Florence, and he observed that the beast had much better sight than man, and a much keener sense of smell. At least these nerves were more efficient than they had been in a man's skull, and the organ of smell had more room in the lion's brain.

Sometimes Leonardo was worried by the lack of opportunity he had to write down all these observations. He made a little apology: "In these (studies) I have been hindered neither by avarice nor by negligence, but simply by want of time." Yet look what he accomplished, even so!

As might be expected, Leonardo thought a good deal about the secret of life itself. As he watched an animal killed at the slaughterhouse, he would wonder just where the spark of life resided in the body. A frog, for example—where was its mainspring? Why was it alive one moment and dead the next? Some injuries killed; others only maimed, and the body got well. Needless to say, Leonardo never satisfied himself on this question.

In the course of his life he dissected the bodies of many sorts of animals as well as human beings. He made a lot of important comparisons between their muscular and skeletal structures. As he did so, he developed a tremendous respect and wonder for life itself. How marvelous was a living body! In cunning and beauty, it outdid the most cunning and beautiful engine that any man could ever contrive. Finally, Leonardo came to a most advanced conclusion—that to destroy life is stupid and wicked.

"Let not your rage or malice destroy a life," he wrote, "for, indeed, he who does not value it, does not himself deserve it."

After this, Leonardo gave up for the rest of his life the invention of murderous weapons and engines.

Even in Florence, there was an end at last to lawsuits. As it became evident that Leonardo's case would soon be finished, he prepared to go back to Milan. Chaumont had begun to get impatient. Leonardo wrote a soothing letter to fix things up: "I have had the feeling that the small return made for the great kindnesses I have received from Your Excellency may have made you annoyed with me." He added that he would be back at Easter time.

There were a lot of things to arrange, mostly practical matters. The King had promised a pension to Leonardo who now asked if it had started to arrive. This time he intended to be independent of Charles d'Amboise in Milan. He would set up on his own, though of course the Viceroy would still be his patron.

When he got back to Milan, he found no dearth of pupils; his housekeeping books show that he had a great number. At last Salai was off the payroll, or should have been. He had set up for himself as a painter of sorts, though he never was as good as he should have been after all his years studying with Leonardo.

However, he was still an expense to Leonardo. Salai's father had become Leonardo's tenant at the vineyard which Lodovico had given him in the last days of Sforza power. But Salai still needed money. Leonardo wrote, "On October . . . 1508 I received 30 gold thalers. I lent 13 to Salai, to make up his sister's dowry, and had 17 left."

However, the King's pension *was* arriving regularly. Leonardo had no worry about his livelihood.

Chapter 10

"THE MEDICI MADE ME AND BROKE ME"

It looked as if Milan would continue to be kind to Leonardo. One of the first commissions after his return should have made him forget his biggest disappointment—the bronze horse of the Sforza. Now another man wanted an equestrian statue. The marshal of

Chaumont's army, a Milanese named Trivulzio, decided that he would provide for his own tomb before he died. He ordered from Leonardo a statue of himself on horseback. It was to be life-size in bronze. This was nothing like the giant statue Lodovico had ordered, but it was a splendid idea, especially as he also wanted the tomb designed by the artist on a grand scale.

Once again Leonardo went happily to work studying horses and making sketches. The problem of the background and the base was complicated. But that was just the sort of thing he enjoyed because it was an engineer's job.

Since he was never satisfied with just one interest at a time, he also turned his attention to his treatise on water. This led him to go on thinking about hydraulics. At the same time he put his studies to practical use, and worked at improving the canal system of Lombardy. He studied the mechanics of locks in these canals. He planned an efficient way to dam the river that flowed past Milan, and a new method for draining swamps.

This led him to study the behavior of water in whirlpools and eddies, as well as "the motion of air imprisoned beneath water." From that he went on to observe eddies of air, little cyclones and great storms. He saw that air was governed by the same laws of behavior that ordered water. "I have seen movements of the air so furious," he wrote, "that they have carried, mixed up in their course, the largest trees of the forest and whole roofs of great palaces, and I have seen the same fury of the air bore a hole with a whirling movement, digging out a gravel pit and carrying gravel, sand, and water more than half a mile through the air."

Those must have been happy days for a man whose only genuine pleasure was in study of this sort. Nobody was pushing Leonardo around any more. He did not have to work too hard at paintings when they began to bore him. He had the means to buy equipment for experiments. He had intelligent patrons who took an interest in the things that interested him.

It is pleasant to think of Leonardo at this time, absorbed in his writing and his thoughts, breaking off work in the studio to watch a river in flood, or a clear night sky full of stars. Now he was fifty-seven years old. At about this time someone painted his portrait. In this he looks older than his age, but very alert and thoughtful.

It was too good to last. Life in sixteenth-century Italy was never peaceful for many years at a stretch. Early in the year 1509, Louis XII came back to prepare for attack in a new war. He rode at the head of a powerful army. This time he was battling the Republic of Venice. Venetian armies were already on the march, aiming for Milan. Louis's Frenchmen, as well as the Milanese, were eager to go out and meet them on the field. Leonardo went with them in his capacity of king's military engineer.

The expedition was successful. And by the time the army returned to Milan, Leonardo had filled a notebook with rapid sketches of landscapes he had seen on the way, and lots of rivers and lakes. He had studied the plumbing system of palaces. He had made friends with Louis's court painter Jean Perreal, like himself a jack-of-all-trades. These two painters discussed engineering, architecture, mathematics and astronomy together.

For one of the celebrations when the army returned to Milan, Leonardo constructed a great mechanical lion that moved around, driving a mechanical dragon out of the sea. The dragon had a fight with a cock—symbol of France—and the cock pecked out its eyes.

Then Leonardo returned contentedly to his studies. All through the winter and until early spring, he worked as he liked. Sometimes he taught in his studio or painted. Sometimes he worked on anatomy, which was again claiming his attention, and at his studies of the stars. But then in 1510 he was interrupted by the next development of the war.

The old Pope, Julius II, had been growing uneasy for some time, as well he might have been, because of the growing power of Louis XII of France. Julius II became definitely worried when Louis defeated the Venetians. It did not suit his ideas to see that powerful Italian state controlled by a French king.

He had always been friendly with the French, but now suddenly, without any warning, he took up the cause of Venice. He enlisted the aid of the Swiss; and though he was a very old man, he went himself to the war. Together the Venetians and the Pope's troops succeeded in beating the French at Correggio. Chaumont, who led the French army, was ill at the time. Shortly after the battle he died, and so Leonardo lost one of the best friends he had ever had.

The French rallied, but the next Viceroy of Milan, too, was promptly killed in battle. Victory passed back and forth, from hand to hand. In the next few years Milan had several masters. Most of Leonardo's friends and patrons were either killed or driven out. Trivulzio, who had ordered the bronze horse for his tomb, fled to France with the retreating army. The tomb was never built.

Leonardo had no income, for now that his friend King Louis was no longer monarch of Milan the pension stopped. Sometimes the Swiss occupied the city, sometimes the Germans. Then one of the Sforza heirs came back to the throne.

Leonardo could not keep pace with these changes.

He had his vineyard still, and his house, but what was he to do for a living? He was more than sixty years old, but a new start was necessary.

It was autumn, 1513. The French had just retired to France, possibly for the last time. Leonardo made up his mind. In September, on the twenty-fourth, he took to the road once more. With his little household of pupils he set out for Rome.

Pope Julius II had died, and Pope Leo X was reigning in his place. This looked as if it would be a fortunate thing for Leonardo, because Leo X was a Medici. Like all his family he was probably interested in the Tuscan painter who had his first chance through the Pope's illustrious father, Lorenzo de Medici. But the two men did not yet know each other well. Rome was practically new territory to Leonardo.

He and his entourage stayed for a while at an inn, but he was soon relieved to get an offer from the Pope to move into the Belvedere. This was honor indeed. The Belvedere was a summer palace belonging to the Church. It was high on the Vatican hill, with a beautiful garden up the slope, approached by a wide marble staircase. There was the Pope's private zoo—just the sort of thing Leonardo loved. It contained lions, panthers, apes, parrots and even a white elephant. Pope Leo X was a great collector. He loved his animals. He also made a collection of rare flowers and herbs and trees. There was an excellent library of ancient books in his palace, and Leonardo was free to study and use all these things.

The Pope's brother Giuliano de Medici lived in Rome. He had already met Leonardo. In spite of the difference in their ages—Giuliano was a young man—they became good friends.

Giuliano was delicate and sickly. He was a philosopher who preferred study and a quiet existence to all other things. His chief interest was literature. He had written some poems in his time, but he was also attracted to the studies of magic and alchemy which men still took very seriously in those days. Leonardo spent a good deal of time rigging up equipment with which his friend pursued experiments along these lines.

It was Giuliano, not the Pope, who paid Leonardo for his living, and made him a generous allowance. Leo X was not exactly stingy, but he wasn't interested in Leonardo's kind of research.

With Giuliano's help the artist fixed up his living quarters in the Belvedere, in apartments that had not been occupied for some time. Everything had to be put in, and everything is listed in the notebooks—partitions, wainscoting, kitchen, windows, a new terrace, furniture, and, most important of all, an elaborate workshop.

In this workshop Leonardo, with the help of a German workman, made mirrors and other things for Giuliano. He made much use of metal screws. Most people of the day did not use screws because they found them too difficult to make, but Leonardo invented thread-cutters that would turn them out without the need of filing them down. His method was devised again, in America, a hundred and fifty years ago.

As things turned out, it was very fortunate for Leonardo that Giuliano de Medici had befriended him. Otherwise he would soon have found himself neglected and crowded out. Rome, the spiritual capital of the world, had long been the place to which all footloose artists turned. Most of the famous painters of Leonardo's generation had tried their luck with the Vatican years before. One in particular, Bramante, was well known to Leonardo because they had worked together in the old days under Lodovico in Milan.

Bramante was an architect and builder. In Rome, while Julius II was alive, he made his name by constructing the buildings the Pope had wanted put up in a great hurry. Bramante was careless, however, and often used material that was not strong, on a design that would not withstand weight and the wear and tear of time.

Though he and Leonardo had known each other very well, he was now too rich and busy and proud to take any notice of the new arrival. He had a protégé in young Raphael. Under Bramante's wing, Raphael got nearly all the plums of commission that the Vatican could offer. When he was hardly more than a youth, he made his fortune. Now in 1510, when Leonardo arrived, Raphael was thirty years old.

Michelangelo was living in Rome also. He had just finished the famous ceiling in the Sistine Chapel. Leonardo went to see it, and he didn't think it so wonderful, after all; he thought all that display of muscles was unnecessary. It was all very well to know your anatomy, but you didn't have to use it in such an exaggerated way, he said. "O painter-anatomist, take care not to become a wooden painter through too strong an emphasis on bones, muscles, and sinews." Michelangelo's figures sometimes look as if they had been flayed alive.

But however much of the old enmity still existed between the two great men, they seem never to have come to open quarreling again. They now moved in very different circles.

Leo X was an unusual Pope. He had a quick mind

and enjoyed strange, interesting things from foreign lands, as, for instance, his animals and plants. But he was not genuinely fond of painting. Naturally, because his brother pressed him to do so, he ordered a painting from Leonardo. But ill-wishers at his court told him that this new painter was experimenting with the varnish (with which all finished pictures were covered for protection) before he had got started on the painting itself. The Pope was at once amused and vexed. He said, "Alas! This man will never get anything done, for he is thinking about the end before he begins." And that was that. Leonardo's career as papal artist was finished.

Leo X much preferred young Raphael, and because he depended on Raphael to do all the painting he wanted, everybody else in Rome followed his example. That was the way the world went. Leonardo was used to being neglected, but no doubt he felt bad about it. However, Raphael was not aggressive or unkind to him, as Michelangelo had been in Florence.

There is an amusing story about these two artists, Michelangelo and Raphael. Michelangelo's passionate nature suffered in Rome, as it had done in Florence, because he wasn't considered the greatest artist of them all. His enmity was now directed at Raphael, naturally, because Raphael was so very successful and rich and

"There you go with your escort!" shouted Michelangelo.

petted by the nobility. Raphael loved to dress in gorgeous clothes and parade through the streets of Rome with his pupils all around him.

One day Michelangelo saw him like this, and took it as a personal insult. He walked up and stood in Raphael's path and shouted, "There you go with your escort, as if you were a general!"

Raphael just smiled and retorted, "And there you

go, all alone like a hangman!" His pupils roared with laughter.

Michelangelo never stopped attacking Raphael, saying that everything the younger man knew had been learned from Michelangelo. Raphael didn't reply to these attacks. He was really an amiable man. And when he mentioned Michelangelo, he was always very polite, admitting that he had learned a good deal from him. Raphael also spoke admiringly of Leonardo, and sometimes gave him jobs to do. But among most of the artists of that world, Leonardo had the reputation of an eccentric, who though he painted like an angel preferred to spend all his time studying some crazy philosophy or other.

In other circumstances Leonardo might have remained in the ruler's good graces by showing his talent for mechanical toys. As it happened, at the papal court Leonardo needed something he did not have—a fluent knowledge of Latin. People around the Pope always spoke Latin. Now Leonardo regretted that as a schoolboy he had refused to study his Latin. He tried to improve his knowledge, but either he was too busy at other things or he just wasn't good at languages. It seems odd that there should have been anything Leonardo couldn't do well.

Besides, he wasn't sympathetic with the sort of thing Leo X liked. The Pope, though a rather young man, was enormously fat. He had his special followers who knew how to amuse him. They all loved silly practical jokes, which like most jokes of that sort were often cruel. He surrounded himself with grotesque men, all jesters. There were a queer little dwarf, and a great fat monk, and others of the sort to share the Pope's sense of humor. All these people were given favors and very good fortunes, but in this company there was no place for Leonardo.

However, he too turned his hand now and then to a joke to amuse the fat, bored Leo X. He made balloons out of wax, in the shape of different animals or funny faces, and flew them in the Vatican gardens. He found an unusual looking lizard one day, and spent hours and hours covering its whole body with scales and attaching to it a beard and horns. He kept it in a box which he would suddenly open when anybody called on him. The little monster would rush out and scare the stranger into fits.

Leonardo loved to stroll in the Papal gardens. There he made a number of careful drawings of the plants and flowers he saw around him. Again these observations brought him to the discovery of natural laws that no one else had seen. He noted that the leaves of different plants grew according to certain consistent rules, in order to get the maximum amount of sunlight even low down on the stem. He found out that you can tell the age of a tree by the number of rings in the trunk's cross section.

He enjoyed the beauty of the flowers and trees. When he wasn't studying them scientifically, he made a lot of observations as to how to paint them. "Remember, O painter, that the variety of depth or shade in any one particular species of plants is in proportion to the rarity or density of their branches. . . . When the sun is in the east the trees are darker toward the middle, while their edges are light."

It was as well that Leonardo had these pursuits, for he seemed to have slipped out of any place in public life. The most outstanding proof of this was that when Isabella d'Este came to Rome, she made no attempt to see him or to get that painting she had wanted for so many years. Instead, she had her portrait painted by Raphael.

Giuliano de Medici's brother had placed him in charge of four cities: Modena, Parma, Piacenza and Reggio. Now he sent Leonardo to Parma, possibly to inspect the fortifications there. On this trip Leonardo also traveled over the Pontine Marshes south of Rome. These marshes were notorious for breeding fever and pestilence. The Pope, perhaps because of his fat, was very subject to fevers, and worried a lot about his health. He was particularly afraid of the marshes.

Giuliano was glad to assent when Leonardo suggested draining them off by digging rivers through them and drying up the land. The work was actually begun, and ended successfully long after both Giuliano and Leonardo were no longer in Rome.

Giuliano was still in his early thirties, but he had the constitution and the habits of an old man. The Pope watched him anxiously, for these brothers were very fond of each other. For some time there had been talk in the Medici family of marrying off Giuliano.

Now the moment seemed to have arrived, when Leo X found a French princess, Philiberta of Savoy, who seemed very suitable. Louis XII was much in favor of marrying this girl to the Pope's brother. She was a hunchback and not very pretty. Giuliano was not keen on getting married in any case, but because the Pope wished it he consented.

Early in January, 1515, Giuliano set out for France. He looked even more ill than usual, and Leonardo could not feel happy about the trip. After seeing the procession off, he went back to his studio, much depressed. With Giuliano out of Rome, it was as if nobody friendly was left.

Leonardo had heard bad news, too: Louis XII had died suddenly. Like many other people, Leonardo needed something tucked away in the back of his brain that could be used as an escape. He had depended on Louis XII; he liked to feel that he would be welcome at the French court, if ever he needed to go. Now that avenue was closed. Unhappily, he wrote, "The Magnifico Giuliano de Medici left Rome on the 9th of January, 1515, just at daybreak, to take a wife in Savoy; and on the same day fell the death of the King of France."

His forebodings were correct. Giuliano had hardly gone when Leonardo began having trouble with Georg, his German assistant in the workshop. The man was surly and impertinent. Without Giuliano to discipline him, he began staying away. He was absent for two months, drinking, and saying he was working at Giuliano's business so Leonardo couldn't order him about. Georg had a friend, another German named Johannes, who worked with him on the mirrors. Johannes, too, turned against Leonardo. The two Germans stole some of Leonardo's inventions and even some of his material for making mirrors.

Like many other scholarly people, Leonardo remained calm in the face of big catastrophes. He never flew off the handle, for instance, when he was forced to move outright from Milan because of the war. But he could not take small annoyances. This petty squabble with workmen sent him into a fit of exasperation. He wrote long complaints against Georg, and was impatient for Giuliano to come back so that he could see justice done. And then to make matters worse he fell ill, and was under a doctor's care for some time.

In the meantime, Giuliano was safely wedded and on his way back. But in Florence he, too, fell ill and had to take to his bed. So Leonardo whiled away the time writing to him, going over the grievances he had against the wicked "German deceiver." Slowly Leonardo recovered. But slow as his cure was, it was faster than that of Giuliano in Florence.

Leonardo filled in the waiting with a sudden spurt of energy, getting his scientific treatises in order, once more, for publication. As always, when he looked over his notes, he found himself starting out on a new series of studies. At first the sketches he made were not so delicate as those in his older style; his sickness, whatever it was, had made him weak and spoiled his control. But in time he got over this and his hand regained its cunning.

Georg ran away rather than face the music when Giuliano was expected home. But Johannes the mirror maker stayed in Rome. He determined to get in some dirty work against Leonardo before judgment should overtake himself. He went to the Pope and complained that Leonardo, during his anatomical studies, had broken the laws of the Church by dissecting human bodies.

Since the days of Pope Boniface VIII there had been a general condemnation of dissection, but there was no law against it. Besides, Leonardo was only one of many people who made scientific studies by this means. For nearly fifty years there had been no complaints from anyone. The Popes who preceded Leo X had not interfered with these studies. The spirit of the Renaissance, the general eagerness for learning, had kept people safe in their researches.

But Leo X was a lazy man, very careful of his position. He was not likely to defend Leonardo against ignorant attacks of this sort, especially with his brother still lying ill in Florence where he couldn't speak up for his favorite.

To justify himself, Leonardo hastily prepared a paper on human speech, with a great number of beautiful drawings illustrating the muscles of the tongue, and the anatomy of the throat and mouth. Through this he hoped to show the value of such scientific studies.

Leonardo handed this in to the Pope's chamberlain, but nobody paid any attention to it. The whole work, with all its careful drawings, was neglected and lost. Leonardo continued to worry about the accusations, and he had reason to do so. It was no light thing to be accused of behaving contrary to church laws. But a greater trouble now pushed all this from the Pope's mind, and also from Leonardo's.

Unlike Julius II, Leo X was no warrior. Indeed, Julius II had been an unusual Pope in his love of fighting. For a long time, Leo X had managed to play off one country against another in his desire to keep the peace, but it was getting harder and harder to do so.

Francis I had succeeded Louis XII as King of France, and he was determined to conquer Milan all over again. The French also demanded Parma and Piacenza, which were presumably under the guardianship of Giuliano. Leo X sent Giuliano at the head of the papal troops to defend these cities. But Giuliano was still not well enough for such an effort. He collapsed before reaching the battlefield, and it became clear that he had not long to live.

When Leo X heard that the French King had retaken Milan, and that the French were triumphantly in charge once more, he hurried to arrange peace at any price. He went all the way to Milan to talk it over with the King.

During the troubled early months of 1516, there is no hint of what Leonardo was doing. He may have been called in to accompany the Pope on his journey, as a man who had lived long in Milan and knew the ways of the French. He may have met the new King; nobody knows. What is certain is that in his enforced idleness he wrote a strange description, out of his vivid imagination, of how to make pictures of the Deluge.

No doubt his long studies of water gave him the inspiration for this. Many of the sketches of his notebooks during these years are of waves, water in turmoil, or land being eaten away by floods. He made a list of things to be remembered in the pictures he described: "darkness, wind, tempest at sea, floods of water, forests on fire, rain, bolts from heaven, earthquakes, and the collapse of mountains, overthrow of cities . . . people on trees which are unable to support them; trees and rocks, towers and hills covered with people; boats, tables, troughs, and other means of floating. Hills covered with men, women, and animals; and lightning from the clouds illuminating everything." For pages he wrote of these catastrophes, and now and then broke off in his writing to illustrate them more vividly.

These thoughts were interrupted by a catastrophe more near to his reality. In March, 1516, Giuliano de Medici died.

Giuliano had been Leonardo's only hope and comfort in Rome. Now he was gone. For a little while the aging painter lingered in the city, but it was clear that he would never get any recognition from Leo X, and only the most grudging help.

Leonardo made up his mind to take for the third time a step which had never failed to bring him relief in his hurt vanity. He would go to Milan, and attach himself to the train of the new French King, Francis I, who was still there.

Farewell to the cheerful, fat, silly Pope Leo X and all his works! Leonardo reflected on Fate, that had made the Medici influence his life so strongly. In his youth Lorenzo neglected him but sent him with a silver lute to try his fortune in Milan with Lodovico il Moro. And now Leonardo was an old man, going to Milan again.

"The Medici made me and broke me," he wrote.

No one who knew him at that moment, when his spirits were at their lowest ebb, could have foreseen that this story would have a happy ending. Yet it was so. Leonardo went to Milan, and there the King, Francis I, gave him the appreciation that was his right. When Francis I went back to France, Leonardo da Vinci was with him—court painter to the King.

Chapter 11

AT THE COURT OF FRANCIS I

The French court was a childish world. The parties the great nobles gave for each other were something like children's parties too. Francis I loved magnificent shows and glittering clothes and all the gaiety he could provide. Leonardo's first mark in France was made at a gathering of this sort in October, 1517.

The King had taken his court to visit his sister Marguerite de Valois, at her castle, Argenton. There was the usual tourney, followed by a play, which was rather like what we call a pageant. It was during the play that Leonardo's talents proved to be so useful.

In one scene of the play, an old hermit came and knelt down before the King and made an elegant, flattering speech. The King had been sent to the world, he said, to save it from a savage lion. As he came to the part about the savage beast, a lion walked in the door and marched down toward the King. Though everyone knew the beast was mechanical, it looked so fierce and snarling that a few silly women screamed. But the King played his part as he was told to do. The hermit gave him a "magic wand" with which he struck the beast. Whereupon the lion reared up; his breast split open and disclosed a turquoise-blue cavity, the color of the French arms. From it fell white lilies—the flowers of France—at the King's feet.

Leonardo often repeated the general idea of his triumph, and he did this at Argenton the next evening. This time, just after dinner, a knight dressed all in gold armor, suddenly appeared in the banqueting hall carrying in front of him a great golden heart. When he put it down before the King, it too opened. The cavity was golden, and there came out from it, not flowers this time but a strange symbolic figure standing on a globe. Half of the figure was a young, vigorous knight; the other half an old, sorrowful man.

What was the meaning of this allegory? The guests whispered to each other and wondered. Leonardo must have explained to them as he did in his notebook: "Pleasure and pain are represented as twins, since there never is one without the other; and as if they were united back to back, since they are contrary to each other . . . Clay, gold . . . If you choose pleasure, know that he has behind him one who will deal you tribulation and repentance."

It may seem to us that this was a queer way to cheer people up at a party, but the courtiers at Argenton took it to heart. The King, for all his wild pursuit of pleasure, was particularly fond of Leonardo in this mood. Besides, he was very much impressed with his painter's knowledge. For the rest of his life he insisted that Leonardo was not only the most learned man he ever met in sculpture, painting and architecture, but a very great philosopher as well.

Francis I treated the old man with courtesy and generosity. He made him a splendid allowance, and also supported Francesco Melzi and Salai. Francis' favorite palace was Amboise on the Loire River. Because he spent so much time at Amboise, he settled Leonardo there. It was to be the painter's last move, and never had he lived in a more congenial place. Francis gave him, for his own home, the villa of Cloux. This was a little chateau hidden away in trees, but with a splendid view of the green countryside.

Leonardo was failing. Though he was only sixty-four, an Italian who came to visit him at Amboise thought he must be well over seventy. This Italian was a young man, traveling as secretary with a Cardinal. He was fascinated as Leonardo talked to the Cardinal and eagerly showed him some of the writings and illustrations that he kept in chests, scattered about the chateau.

Leonardo told him he had dissected more than thirty corpses in his life, and he exhibited his drawings of anatomical studies. The young secretary looked with awe at all the hundreds of books packed away, still unpublished. "If they come to light they will be valuable and very delightful," he wrote later.

At about this time Leonardo had a stroke that crippled his right hand so badly that he couldn't use it to paint with. People took it for granted that he was finished as an artist. He might still plan pictures and tell his pupils how to fill them in, they thought, but that was all. They forgot, or never knew, that Leonardo was one of those rare people who are called ambidextrous. He could use his left hand as well as his right. Therefore, though he no longer painted entire pictures by himself, he was still capable of blocking out the drawing, and painting the important bits of the picture afterwards. In that way, no doubt, he painted his last great work, "Saint John the Baptist."

Francis I was so fond of talking to Leonardo that, whenever he was in residence at Amboise, he would come to Cloux every day. There he would sit and talk and talk and talk. He had magnificent plans, and though he had a way of forgetting all about them in pursuit of some new idea, it gave Leonardo pleasure to pretend that these projects would someday come true.

Francis wanted to pull down his castle and build a new and better one, so Leonardo drew up the pattern for it, and seems to have hoped that it would be built. He traveled around with the King. During this time he invented transportable, or prefabricated, houses. He persuaded Francis to consider a canal system that would unite some of the big cities of France. Again he dreamed of draining marshes and making good soil out of useless swamp.

The last great festivities that Leonardo was ever to assist in took place in May, 1518. Two occasions were being celebrated: the baptism of the Dauphin, the son of Francis I, and the wedding of young Lorenzo de Medici to a French princess.

This time there was a tourney that lasted a whole week. Then the castle square was disguised with painted scenery of towers and walls, so that it looked like a fortified city. One of the highlights was a mock bombardment. Wooden cannon shot enormous balls across the scene. The cannon balls bounced about merrily because they were hollow and harmless. Francis led the attack on the city, urging his knights to follow bravely. From within the mock fortress came the "besieged" garrison. There was a lifelike fight in the square, during which several people were actually killed in the excitement.

One social occasion followed another. Leonardo remembered the success of his blue canvas sky in the castle at Milan, and built one like it, with planets moving around the edge and the sun and the moon above. As nobody there had ever seen it before, the French exclaimed at this wonder.

That winter was a hard, cold one, and Leonardo missed the Italian sun. A long time before his death, he knew what was happening. The old urge to put down on record all that he knew had begun to ebb. On April 23, 1519, he sent for a notary and made his will. Leonardo had always been precise and businesslike when he wanted to be. He was very calm and efficient about this will. To his brothers in Florence, in spite of the quarrels they had had, he left the money he had in that city and property he had acquired in Fiesole.

To Francesco Melzi, who was always there at his bedside, faithful to the last, he bequeathed all his books and paintings and instruments, as well as the money he had in the house, and that still due to him from the King. All his clothing, too, went to Melzi (clothing was very valuable) except for one cloak lined with fur and a cap to go with it, which he gave to his serving-woman.

Half his Milanese vineyard and some money due to him from the allowance made by Louis II went to a servant, and the other half of the vineyard to Salai, who had already built a house and was living there.

For witnesses, Leonardo had five priests of the neighborhood. He had never pretended to be a religious man. But now as many people do, he thought of the meaning of death, and he turned to God.

In his old businesslike manner, after he had made his confession, he planned his burial ceremonies. They were to include so many High Masses, so many Low, and ten pounds of thick wax candles. Sixty poor peo-

Leonardo wept over the tasks he was leaving unfinished.

ple, each carrying a torch, were to walk behind his coffin from Cloux to Amboise, where he was to be buried. It wouldn't take long to make this walk, even slowly, said Leonardo, and the torches would not be used up. Afterwards the torches could be distributed among the four churches of the hamlet. Though he was so careful about the little matter of the torches, Leonardo made no mention or design of a memorial stone for his grave.

Just before the end he was overcome with sorrow

at the thought of all the tasks he had left undone, and all the paintings that should have been better. He had not published anything, not a thing. At the thought of all this waste, the tears ran down his cheeks. Melzi could not comfort him.

At last, on May 2, 1519, the end came to Leonardo da Vinci at the age of sixty-seven. He died convinced that he had accomplished nothing.

INDEX

Alfonso of Aragon, 64
Amboise, 169-71, 174
Ambrogio de Predis, 47-49
Anatomy, Leonardo's study of, 55, 138-44
Animals, Leonardo's studies of, 143-144
in zoo of Leo X, 151
Arezzo, 92
Argenton, 168
Arno River, 103, 105, 109
Artisan, fifteenth-century role of, 17-18

Baroncelli, Bernardo de Bandino, 27-29
"Battle of Anghiari," 105, 115, 118, 122, 132
Beatrice d'Este, 57-60, 64-65, 74-75
Belvedere palace, 151-52
Bianca Maria, 59-60
Birds, Leonardo's studies of, 102, 118-19, 122-24
Boniface VIII, 163
Botticelli, 5, 28-29
Bramante, 153-54
Buonarroti, Michelangelo, *see* Michelangelo Buonarroti

Canal(s), engineered by Leonardo, 94-95, 103-05
overflow of, 109
Cannon, Leonardo's interest in, 31-32, 43
Cartoon, as preliminary drawing, 89
Cesare Borgia, 90-97
Cesena, 94-95
Charles VIII, 63-64, 66-67, 74, 93
Chaumont, Sire de (Viceroy of Milan), 125-27, 130-33, 144-45, 150
Cloux, 170-71, 174
Columbus, Christopher, 4, 9
Constantinople, 18, 64
Copernicus, 9
Cosimo de Medici, 18

da Vinci, Leonardo, *see* Leonardo da Vinci
d'Amboise, Charles, 135, 145
"David," 110-12
Dissections, Church laws against, 163
by Leonardo, 55, 138-44
Drawings, Leonardo's:
of anatomical studies, 140-42, 163, 170
of landscapes, 149
of plants, 158
of war machines, 41-42
Duomo cathedral, 27

Fiesole, 124-25, 173
Firearms, Leonardo's interest in, 31-32, 42
Florence, 3-4, 6-7, 11, 14, 19, 87-89, 97, 125, 128, 162
beauty of, 18
canal built near, 105
overflow of, 109
and Cesare Borgia, 93, 95
goldsmiths in, 17
Greek culture in, 18
and Leonardo, 14, 18-26, 28-37, 87-90, 97, 102-25, 134-35, 136-141, 142-44
Leonardo's dislike of, 35
letter from Signoria criticizing Leonardo, 127
Medici rule of, 16
and Michelangelo, 110*ff*.
Milan different from, 38

Naples in war with, 31, 33-34
Pisa in war with, 103-04
processions in, 24-26
scholars in, Leonardo's views on, 35-36
tourneys in, 24-26
and Vitellozzo Vitelli, 92-93, 95
wealth of, 17
Flying, Leonardo's interest in, 97-103, 119, 122-25
Flying machine, Leonardo's designs of, 100-02, 119, 123-24
France, Leonardo's last years in, 167-75
Francesco da Vinci, 108, 134
Francesco Gonzaga, 79, 81, 83
Francesco Melzi, 133, 169, 173, 175
Francesco Sforza, statue of, 39, 46, 50-51, 53, 58-59, 61, 67-68, 76-77
Michelangelo's comment on, 113-115
Francis I (King of France), 164-173
court of, Leonardo's creations at, 168-69, 172

Geometry, Leonardo's interest in, 88-89
Genoa, 130-31
Georg, 161-62
Giacomo (Salai), 56, 79, 133, 145, 169, 173
Gian Galeazzo Sforza, 37, 49, 51, 64-65
Giuliano de Medici (Lorenzo's brother), 26-27
Giuliano de Medici (Pope Leo's brother), 152-53, 160-62, 164-165
Goldsmiths, Florentine, 17
Gunnery, Leonardo's interest in, 31-32, 42

Hydraulics, Leonardo's study of, 66, 147

Imola, 95, 97
Isabella of Aragon, 49, 51, 59-60, 64, 75
Isabella d'Este, 79-83, 89-90, 132, 159
Italy, division of, 15-16

Johannes, 161-62
Julius II, 149-51, 153, 164

"Last Supper, The," 71-73, 76, 78, 84
"Leda and the Swan," 121
Leo X, 151, 154-55, 157-65
Leonardo da Vinci:
abilities of, varied, 40-43
Ambrogio in partnership with, 47-49
anatomy studied by, 55. 138-44
animals studied by, 143-44
appearance of, 6, 87
as apprentice to Verrocchio, 18-23, 26
apprentices of, 56
architecture studied by, 54, 93
in Arezzo, 92
Baroncelli's body sketched by, 28-29
birds observed by, 102, 122
treatise on flight of, 118-19
birth of, 4, 8
birthplace of, 4
boyhood of, 6-7, 11-14
canal(s) engineered by, 94-95, 103-105
overflow of, 109
castle decorated by, 49-50
Cesare Borgia as patron of, 90*ff*.
at court of Francis I, 167-69
pageants devised by, 168-69, 172
curiosity of, 8
death of, 175
Deluge described by, 165
designs and inventions, of bomb, 42

of bridges, 40
of cannon, 31, 43
of diving suit, 85-86
of flame thrower, 42
of flying machine, 100-02, 119, 122-24
of grenade, 42
of grinding plants, 70
of guns, 31, 42
of lamp, 55-56
of lift, 104
of lute, 37
of needle-shaping machine, 69
of parachute, 101
of Paradise Festival, 52-53
of prefabricated houses, 171
of printing press, 138
of revolving-scythe machine, 42
of rolling machines, 70
of spinning wheel, 69
of submarine, 86-87
of tank, 42
of telescope, 107
of thread-cutters, 153
of treadmill, 104
of weapons of war, 31-33, 40-43, 85-87
dissections by, 55, 138-44, 163
drawings of, *see* Drawings, Leonardo's
dress of, 87-88
as engineer, 84-85, 87, 91, 94, 103, 135, 149
father of, 6, 11-12, 14, 18-19, 28, 88
will of, 107-08, 134
at fifty-seven, 148
in Florence, 14, 18-26, 28-37, 87-90, 97, 102-25, 134-44
and Florentine scholars, views on, 35-36
and flying, childhood memory in regard to, 98-99
interest in, 97-103, 119, 122-125
at forty-eight, 87
fossils observed by, 7, 9, 21
in France, 167-75
frictional effects observed by, 70
genius of, 5-6
geometry studied by, 88-89
German assistants troublesome to, 161-62
and Giacomo (Salai), 56, 79, 133, 145, 169, 173
and Giuliano de Medici, 152-53
gravity studied by, 65
as heir, 108
hydraulics studied by, 66, 147
in Imola, 95
intellect of, 6, 8
interests of, varied, 5-6, 21, 83, 107
inventions and designs, *see* designs and inventions
and Isabella d'Este, 82-83
"Last Supper, The," painted by, 71-73, 76, 78, 84
Latin neglected by, 157
lawsuit by, 134-35, 144
light and vision studied by, 54-55
list of abilities drawn up by, 40-43
Lodovico as patron of, 53*ff*.
Madonnas painted by, 32
in Mantua, 79, 82
marshes drained by, 92
mathematics studied by, 20
mechanical ability of, 32, 69-70
and Michelangelo, 112-17
in Milan, 37-40, 45-60, 64-76, 78, 102, 126-33, 145-50, 166
as military engineer, 84-85, 87, 91, 94, 103, 149
modernity of, 8
"Mona Lisa" painted by, 119-22
notebooks of, 5, 21, 41, 46, 65, 69, 72, 86, 107, 122, 139-40, 149, 152
as painter, 6, 32, 34-35, 71-74, 83-84, 88-89, 105-06, 109-10, 115-120
painting ruined by fire, 118
in Parma, 159

in Pavia, 53-54
and pension by Louis XII, 145, 150
in Piobino, 92
plants observed by, 158-59
poison gas discovered by, 43
in Rome, 151-65
at Rustici's house, 135-38
"Saint John the Baptist" painted by, 171
and Salai (Giacomo), 56, 79, 133, 145, 169, 173
schooling of, early, 6-7
shield decorated by, 12-14
at sixty, 151
at sixty-four, 170
slowness of, 32-33, 47-48, 58, 106-107, 115
sorrow over unfinished tasks, 174-175
and statue of Francesco Sforza, 39, 46, 50-51, 53, 58-59, 61, 67-68, 76-77
Michelangelo's comment on, 113-15
steam power discovered by, 43
stepmother of, 12
as storyteller, 57-58
strength of, 87
stroke suffered by, 170-71
studies of, as apprentice, 20-21
in Pavia library, 54
in Pope Leo's library, 152
uncle of, 108, 134
in Urbino, 93
in Venice, 83-87
vineyard of, 75, 145, 151, 173
viniculture studied by, 75
vision and light studied by, 54-55
will of, 173-74
Ligny, Count de, 84
Lodovico Sforza, 39, 43, 46, 48, 50-51, 58, 66, 70-71, 73
and Bianca Maria, 59-60
and Charles VIII, 63-64, 67, 74
dark complexion of, 37
death of, 78
defeated by French, 76, 78
as Duke of Milan, 65
as Leonardo's patron, 53*ff.*
Leonardo's pay stopped by, 68
marriage of, 57
vineyard given to Leonardo, 75, 145
wife's death, 74
Loggia dei Lanzi, 111-12
Lorenzo de Medici, 16-19, 24-27, 31, 33-37, 151
Louis of Orleans (later Louis XII), 66-67, 74-76
Louis XII (King of France), 78, 89-90, 93-94, 126-28, 130-35
death of, 160-61
Leonardo admired by, 76, 128
pension awarded to Leonardo, 145
in war with Venice, 148-50

Macchiavelli, 91, 95, 103, 109
Mantua, 79
Mathematics, and art, 20
Maximilian I, 59, 67
Medici family, Florence ruled by, 16
Medici tomb, 4
Mercenary troops, use of, 33-34
Michelangelo Buonarroti, 5, 118, 139
"David" by, 110-12
Leonardo insulted by, 113-15
Raphael attacked by, 155-57
in Rome, 154-57
Milan, 37, 84, 93-94, 125-29
beauty of, 38
cloth-making in, 69
Florence different from, 38
French conquest of, 76, 78, 164
and Leonardo, 37-40, 45-60, 64-76, 78, 102, 126-32, 145, 166
happiness of, 128-29, 131-33, 148-49
steel-making in, 69
wealth of, 38
"Mona Lisa," 119-22
Motion and Weight, 76
Mural painting, 115-17

INDEX

Naples:
  conquest by Charles VIII, 64
  French claim to, 93
  King of, in war against Florence, 31, 34
  recapture by allies, 67
Notebooks, Leonardo's, 5, 21, 46, 65, 69, 86, 139-40, 149, 152
  allegory explained in, 169
  anatomical studies recorded in, 139-41
  father's death mentioned in, 107
  flying machine described in, 122
  gravity as subject of, 65
  and "Last Supper, The," 72
  sketches in, 41, 140-41, 149

Painting:
  fifteenth-century importance of, 9-10
    and photographic function, 10, 28
  mural, 115-17
  in oil, 20
  in tempera, 20
Palace of the Signoria, in Florence, 111
Palazzo Vecchio, 27
Paper-making, 8
Paradise Festival, 52-53
Parma, 159, 164
Patrons of art, 36
Pavia, 53-54
Pazzi family, 27, 31
Perreal, Jean, 149
Perspective, in art, 10-11, 20
Piacenza, 159, 164
Piero da Vinci (Ser Piero), 6, 11-12, 14, 18-19, 28, 88
  will of, 107-08, 134
Piombino, 92
Pisa, 103-04, 109
Pitti Palace, 4
Plague, 25
Pontine Marshes, 159
Pope:
  and Lodovico, 67
  and Lorenzo, 31
  See also Julius II; Leo X
Prince, The, 91
Printing, invention of, 8

Raphael, 154-57, 159
Renaissance, 8, 10, 90, 139, 163
Romagna, 92, 94
Rome:
  and Leonardo, 151-65
  and Michelangelo, 154-57
  and Raphael, 154-57, 159
Rustici, 135-38

"Saint John the Baptist," 171
Salai (Giacomo), 56, 79, 133, 145, 169, 173
Santa Maria delle Grazie, monastery of, 71, 76
Sculpture, fifteenth-century importance of, 9-10
Skeleton, Leonardo's study of, 140-141
Sketches, *see* Drawings
Spain, King of, 67
Swan Mountain, 124-25

Tempera, 20
Tourneys, 24-26
Treatise on Painting, 74
Trivulzio, 147, 150
Turks, 84-85
Tuscany, 3, 19, 26

Urbino, 93
Urbino, Duke of, 95

Valois, Marguerite de, 168
Venice, 83-85, 87, 148-50
  Doge of, 67
Verrocchio, Andrea del, 19-23, 26
Vinci, Leonardo da, *see* Leonardo da Vinci
Vinci, village of, 4, 11, 14
"Virgin and Saint Anne, The," 89
Vitellozzo Vitelli, 92-93, 95

Zoo, of Leo X, 151

Landmark
BOOKS